PERCEPTUAL-MOTOR ACTIVITIES FOR CHILDREN

An Evidence-Based Guide to Building Physical and Cognitive Skills

Jill A. Johnstone

Molly Ramon

Human Kinetics

Library of Congress Cataloging-in-Publication Data

Johnstone, Jill A.
  Perceptual-motor activities for children : an evidence-based guide to building physical and cognitive skills / Jill A. Johnstone, Molly Ramon.
    p. cm.
  Includes bibliographical references.
  ISBN-13: 978-1-4504-0154-8 (soft cover)
  ISBN-10: 1-4504-0154-6 (soft cover)
  1. Perceptual-motor learning--Handbooks, manuals, etc. 2. Activity programs in education--Handbooks, manuals, etc. 3. Teaching--Aids and devices--Handbooks, manuals, etc. I. Ramon, Molly. II. Title.
  LB1067.J57 2011
  370.15'5--dc22

                    2011009280

ISBN-10: 1-4504-0154-6 (print)
ISBN-13: 978-1-4504-0154-8 (print)

The Web addresses cited in this text were current as of March 2011, unless otherwise noted.

Acquisitions Editor: Scott Wikgren; **Developmental Editor:** Jacqueline Eaton Blakley; **Assistant Editors:** Bethany J. Bentley and Anne Rumery; **Copyeditor:** Tom Tiller; **Permissions Manager:** Dalene Reeder; **Graphic Designer:** Joe Buck; **Graphic Artist:** Dawn Sills; **Cover Designer:** Keith Blomberg; **Photographer (cover):** Sara Riggs; **Photographers (interior):** Jill A. Johnstone and Molly Ramon; **Art Manager:** Kelly Hendren; **Associate Art Manager:** Alan L. Wilborn; **Illustrations:** © Human Kinetics; **Printer:** Versa Press

Printed in the United States of America   10 9 8 7 6 5 4 3 2 1

The paper in this book is certified under a sustainable forestry program.

Human Kinetics
Web site: www.HumanKinetics.com

United States: Human Kinetics
P.O. Box 5076
Champaign, IL 61825-5076
800-747-4457
e-mail: humank@hkusa.com

Canada: Human Kinetics
475 Devonshire Road Unit 100
Windsor, ON N8Y 2L5
800-465-7301 (in Canada only)
e-mail: info@hkcanada.com

Europe: Human Kinetics
107 Bradford Road
Stanningley
Leeds LS28 6AT, United Kingdom
+44 (0) 113 255 5665
e-mail: hk@hkeurope.com

Australia: Human Kinetics
57A Price Avenue
Lower Mitcham, South Australia 5062
08 8372 0999
e-mail: info@hkaustralia.com

New Zealand: Human Kinetics
P.O. Box 80
Torrens Park, South Australia 5062
0800 222 062
e-mail: info@hknewzealand.com

E5290

CONTENTS

PREFACE

Educators who want to help children develop to their full potential must educate the whole child by addressing physical, mental, and emotional needs. Many programs at elementary schools focus on academic and emotional development, but how many address children's physical development?

It is increasingly clear that giving short shrift to children's physical development gives short shrift to children. In fact, more and more modern research shows that programs focused on improving children's physical skills enhance not only their physical health but also their academic and emotional health!

We are elementary physical education teachers who created one such program—a perceptual-motor learning laboratory (PMLL). We attended workshops, contacted experts in the field, and researched the topic. We then built a blueprint for a perceptual-motor learning laboratory and implemented it at our school. For the past 6 years, we have been using, refining, and improving the program, which has been so successful that it has been integrated into another 45 schools! What kind of success have we seen? Consider the following example.

In the 2007–2008 school year, our kindergarten physical education classes included twin boys. Each twin, who for the sake of our story will be called Allen and Benny, had a different classroom teacher. By watching the twins' behaviors around their peers in a regular physical education environment, we observed that Allen, the dominant twin, was more socially advanced than Benny. When we tested the boys in our motor lab, we also found that Allen scored 19 points higher than Benny did on the gross motor test. Both boys were still developing on their reading readiness test, but Benny's lower gross motor score qualified him for our lab, whereas Allen's score did not.

At the end of our 32-week program, the reading readiness test results were made available to parents, and the boys' mother came to school with great concern because even as Benny had passed his reading readiness test and tremendously improved his scores on the gross motor test, Allen's scores had stayed the same. As a result, the boys' mother began to question the competence of Allen's teacher.

When this concern was brought to our principal, we were asked to look into the pretest and post-test scores, and we found that Benny had improved by 52 points. When the twins had been pretested for their gross motor skills, Allen had scored a 91 and Benny a 72. These scores tell us that Benny was functioning at or below 3 years of age in locomotor and object-control skills, whereas Allen was functioning at his appropriate age level. However, when these boys were post-tested (by professors at the University of Texas San Antonio to avoid bias), Benny's score rose from 72 to 124, but Allen's remained at 91. Furthermore, Benny passed his reading readiness test, but Allen did not.

Our principal reminded the boys' mother about Benny's participation in our lab, and they discussed Benny's improvements. The boys' mother informed us that there had also been a complete role reversal in the twins' behavior. Benny had become the "alpha twin," and in fact Allen is still trying to catch up.

This is only one success story about children in our lab, and it is particularly persuasive since it offers a comparison of two children raised in the same environment by the same parents. We have written *Perceptual-Motor Activities for Children* so that you can achieve similar results in your classroom. This easy-to-use guide shows you how to build your own perceptual-motor learning laboratory by using equipment that you most likely already have in your facility, as well as a few items that you can create and customize. It will take some work, but a lot of it is fun (e.g., building special mats and creating activity stations). You will also need some help, but volunteers who learn how effective the program is can be quickly won over to the effort—an effort that can change the lives of the children you teach.

WHY DO KIDS NEED PERCEPTUAL-MOTOR EXPERIENCES?

Perceptual-motor skills allow sensory information to be successfully obtained and understood with appropriate reaction. *Perceptual* deals with obtaining information and *motor* refers to the outcome of movement. Thus perceptual-motor activities require children to use their brain and body together to accomplish tasks—for example, walking on a balance beam while reciting the alphabet.

Think about it: To perform well in school, children must do many things that require their mind and muscles to work together as a team. In fact, all communication skills—reading, writing, speaking, and gesturing—are motor-based abilities. We often think of them strictly as academic skills, but, for example, in learning to write, a child must not only know the alphabet and understand how words are formed by combining letters but also translate that knowledge into action by gripping, moving, and stabilizing a pencil while using perception (sight) to adjust her or his movements in order to create the correct pattern. In order for the child to learn, the mind and the body must work together.

Participation in perceptual-motor activities enables students to develop greater levels of body control and encourages greater effort in all areas of the school curriculum. Young students who possess adequate perceptual-motor skills enjoy better coordination, greater body awareness, stronger intellectual skills, and a more positive self-image. In contrast, students who lack these skills often struggle with coordination, possess poor body awareness, and feel less confident. Research also shows that perceptual-motor development is critical to children's development of brain pathways that cross the right and left hemispheres. Because of this, students with poor perceptual-motor development often experience difficulty in learning to read and write when they are in the primary grades. Enhancing gross motor ability by using lateralities to help develop neural pathways in the brain improves a child's ability to read and write. Reading and writing are motor-based abilities that require the mind and body to work together. Students who have not been introduced to proper movement (e.g., running, jumping, throwing, catching) tend to have problems cognitively because the pathways in the brain have not been developed. The optimal time to develop these pathways is between ages 3 and 6.

Perceptual-motor activities provide a proven way to improve children's health and learning in all aspects, and our research shows that students who participate in our program demonstrate significant improvement in all areas of the learning process. Meeting a child's gross motor needs improves his or her academic readiness and overall behavior. Our students with learning disabilities also show improvement that helps them reach their full potential. In 2009, for example, a first-grade student who was totally nonverbal joined our program on a referral from the campus speech therapist. By the end of the year, the student was reading, writing, and talking in complete sentences. He improved his academic performance tremendously and practiced better self-control when interacting socially with classmates. By moving and learning at the same time, this student developed connections in his brain that established pathways and thus increased his confidence and academic success.

Physical activity builds neural pathways—the connections by which information travels through the brain—and a child whose brain has more neural pathways will be able to learn more easily. It is crucial that we help our children develop perceptual-motor skills. These skills are necessary for preparing a child's brain to learn; when a child does not properly develop them, he or she will experience difficulty in learning the basic academic skills of reading and writing. Thus a child who has sufficient perceptual-motor skills will be more prepared to learn and will enjoy better coordination and improved self-image. Perceptual-motor experiences build a strong base to support future academic learning. Early intervention is crucial!

WHAT IS THE PERCEPTUAL-MOTOR LEARNING LABORATORY?

The perceptual-motor learning laboratory involves a 32-week program of sequential station activities meant to enhance children's development of perceptual-motor learning in order to meet their academic needs as young learners. The program addresses physical growth and is designed to target individual development of motor skills for young students who are lagging behind in this critical area of development. The PMLL allows young learners to engage in gross motor behavior through activities that are meaningful, purposeful, and carefully sequenced in an eight-station format using a variety of common and specially designed equipment. The first 8 weeks of lessons involve bilateral activity, the second 8 weeks address unilateral activity, and the third 8 weeks cover cross-lateral activities. The final 8 weeks are dedicated to stations requiring the use of a variety of lateralities. Students participate in the lab at least four times a week for 30 minutes during each session.

The program typically targets the following components of perceptual-motor development for intervention:

- Laterality (through unilateral, bilateral, and cross-lateral activities)
- Balance
- Body image
- Tracking
- Spatial relations
- Locomotor skills (e.g., walking, running, jumping, hopping, galloping, leaping)
- Manipulative skills (e.g., bouncing, catching, dribbling, kicking, tossing, rolling, throwing)

The program begins with a screening process to assess the child's current levels of gross motor development and reading readiness. The screening identifies students who are most at risk and establishes baselines for measuring participants' improvement after they complete the program. At the end of the program, it is expected that participants will demonstrate gains in perceptual-motor development and academic readiness. We determine these gains by reviewing and cross-referencing scores from a reading assessment given by the classroom teacher and a gross motor assessment given by the physical education teacher or the lab instructor. The results for our program participants (our motor lab students) as compared with results for the control group (all other kindergarteners) demonstrate the success of the lab—and yours will too!

USING THIS GUIDE TO BUILD A PMLL

This book and the accompanying online resource provide the road map for duplicating our success in your own teaching environment. Although the program is mainly geared toward elementary school teachers, its principles can be adapted for smaller environments, such as preschools or daycare facilities.

Chapter 1 gives you the nuts-and-bolts information you need in order to implement a PMLL. From getting administrative support to building stations to assessing participants' progress, this chapter outlines the who, what, when, where, and why of getting your program up and running. It features a simple skill assessment test—including photos of correct technique and a ready-to-use record sheet—that you can use as a screening tool.

Chapters 2 through 5 describe 200 illustrated station activities to use in your PMLL. The lab begins with bilateral activities (chapter 2) that require students to use both sides of the body in doing the same thing at the same time—for example, jumping jacks. Chapter 3 focuses on unilateral activities, in which students concentrate on using one side of the body. Chapter 4 addresses cross-lateral activities, which require students to execute movements that cross the body's midline. Chapter 5 closes the program with activities that combine all lateralities. Chapters 2-4 include 8 weeks of activities in an eight-station format. Chapter 5 provides the culminating activities (for the final 8 weeks) and the wrap-up for the 32-week program. The first week of combined lateralities is an example week, but can be used for two weeks. If time permits, instructors may go back and combine their favorite activities to make their own obstacle course stations.

The activities are short and simple to set up, and they use a variety of equipment to keep students interested and challenged. They incorporate academic skill in the form of *active learning cards*, which show letters, shapes, pictures, numbers, and sight words. These full-color cards can be printed from the online resource that accompanies this book and placed inside clear sleeves on cones or mats. As students do the activities using the cones and mats, they say what is shown on the cards, which requires them to practice using their mind and muscles together to meet each challenge.

WEB RESOURCE

The web resource that accompanies this book is available at www.HumanKinetics.com/PerceptualMotorActivitiesForChildren and includes the following elements that you can use in your PMLL:

- Complete set of active learning cards that can be printed and used in the station activities

- Activity cards for each activity used in the PMLL (Each station activity is presented in activity card format in the book and the online resource. You can print the activity cards from the online resource and post them at the stations in order to assist you and other helpers with setting up the stations and checking skill execution while students are doing the activities.)

- Extra perceptual-motor activities not included in the book (We have developed a curriculum using the mats and active learning cards. These activities can also be used in a classroom station setting. Most early learning classrooms include stations, and the mat curriculum is an exciting way to incorporate moving and learning into the classroom setting. The mat activities can also be used as replacements for equipment the lab instructors may not have in their equipment rooms. These mats are easy to construct, set up, and store.)

- Skill assessment record sheet for screening data

- Instructions for building mats and other equipment to use in the lab

- Note that you can send to parents of children you would like to include in the program

- Floor pattern cards to be used with the activities on pages 79 and 99

- Station music that you can download to play during the lab activity in order to keep students engaged and cue them to move to a new station

We hope to help you give young students every chance to be their best by providing them with the opportunity—in a motor laboratory—to develop physically, socially, emotionally, and intellectually. The results we've seen in our perceptual-motor learning laboratory, and in those that have been modeled on it, speak for themselves. We offer this book and online resource as a reliable guide to building a program that will help you prepare your students for a lifetime of learning.

ACKNOWLEDGMENTS

We would like to recognize the following individuals:

Linda Seewald, our physical education district supervisor, for lending her expertise in the field of motor development and her belief in our program

Judy Rosanno, our principal, for asking us to develop the program and opening the door for us to implement a motor lab in our school

Dr. Robbi Beyer, an expert in the field of motor development and motor laboratories, for her support and knowledge

BUILDING A PERCEPTUAL-MOTOR LEARNING LABORATORY

Excellent preparation will put you well on your way to running an excellent perceptual-motor learning laboratory (PMLL). This chapter explores logistical factors that you will need to consider in building your lab, such as acquiring equipment and conducting screenings. It also shows you how to use this book and its accompanying online resource to facilitate your work as you prepare and run your lab.

PLANNING YOUR LABORATORY

To get your laboratory off to a great start and ensure that it runs smoothly, it's important to plan ahead! Doing so involves thinking about how you're going to ensure that you have all the support and resources that you will need for the program.

First, settle some fundamental logistical questions—for example, when and where? We've found it best to conduct the PMLL in the morning, for the first 30 minutes of the school day, at least 4 days a week. The best location is the gym, since it includes most of the needed equipment and provides plenty of space. However, another large multipurpose room, such as a cafeteria or empty classroom or portable building, can also work. Something is better than nothing, and it's OK to start small if your resources are initially limited.

When proposing a perceptual-motor learning laboratory to your administration and parents, it is a good idea to let them know what the lab is, how it works, who would benefit, and what participants would gain (academic readiness). It is also important to address the best time to run the PMLL and why it is crucial for this program to be implemented. The best time to run the lab is in the morning, for the first 30 minutes of school, so you'll need to coordinate with administration to make that time available.

Make sure parents and administrators understand why motor development is important at an early stage and explain its correlation with reading development. Children rely on motor development to obtain, understand, and react successfully to sensory information. Young students with adequate motor skills have improved coordination, increased body awareness, stronger intellectual skills, and a more positive self-image when compared with peers who have inadequate motor skills. In contrast, students lacking these skills often struggle with coordination, have poor body awareness, and are less confident. Additionally, research shows that motor development is critical to the development of brain pathways that cross the right and left hemisphere. Because of this, students with poor perceptual-motor development often have difficulty learning to read and write when they are in the primary grades. To develop to their full potential, it is important that we look at the whole child and address their physical, mental, and emotional needs. There are many programs that focus on academic and emotional needs; however, a motor development program addresses physical growth and it is designed to target individual development of motor skills for young students who may be lagging behind in this critical area of development.

Figure 1.1 shows a sample letter to parents explaining the program; it is available for downloading from the web resource.

Staffing for a PMLL can pose a challenge. Is it necessary to have help when running a lab? No—but if it is possible to find extra hands, do it. Typically, once staff members hear about the success of students involved in the PMLL, they will volunteer to help. We have even had our top fifth-grade students come in to help!

It is not necessary for helpers to possess any physical education expertise. Each activity is presented in a format that can be posted as an activity card indicating key skill criteria for the activity, so anyone can consult the list and easily assess students' performance. (You can access all the activities in the web resource to easily download and print the cards you need; you could also copy them from the book.)

PREPARING EQUIPMENT

Many of the PMLL activities use common equipment that you may already have in your gym or be otherwise able to access easily. Here are some examples:

Floor balance beam

Beanbags

Cones (with plastic sleeves to hold active learning cards)

Foam hurdles (14 inches high)

Gymnastics mats

Hoops (30 inches in diameter) and hoop holders (made out of foam with a slit to hold the hoop)

Juggling scarves (Juggling scarves are a specific size, weight, and color, as compared with other types of scarves. If juggling scarves are not available, plastic grocery bags may be used.)

Jump ropes

Playground balls

Student's name: _____

Classroom teacher: _____

Please read the following and sign at the bottom of this page.

Your child is invited to participate in our perceptual-motor learning lab. A child's proper brain function depends on the early development of locomotor skills (e.g., running, jumping, hopping, galloping, sliding, and leaping) and object control skills (e.g., catching, rolling, hitting, dribbling, throwing, and kicking) that affect learning. Our perceptual-motor learning lab involves a planned sequence of learning and motor experiences designed to help each child reach his or her full potential. It sets aside time for young students to engage in structured and sequentially developed activities that concentrate on the body's lateralities to develop pathways in the brain. Developing pathways by using bilateral activities, which use both sides of the body at the same time; unilateral activities, which isolate one side of the body at a time; and cross-lateral activities, which use the body in opposition, enhances a child's cognitive development.

Here are several ways in which your student could benefit from participating in our perceptual-motor learning lab, which consists of station activities designed to improve your child's academic and gross motor development:

1. Gross motor responses reinforce learning.
2. Eye–hand coordination gained through motor skills helps a child write better.
3. Creating movement in a series helps students develop their ability to read and spell.
4. Movement increases heart rate and circulation, which, in turn, increase a child's performance, narrow his or her attention to target tasks, and increase oxygen supply to his or her key brain areas.
5. Activity enhances spatial relations (i.e., a child's awareness of his or her body's position in space).
6. Certain kinds of movement can stimulate the child's body to release natural motivators. These chemical messengers, known as neurotransmitters, play a primary role in the child's ability to learn.

Your child has been selected to participate in our perceptual-motor learning lab after a review of his or her scores on the TPRI Early Reading Assessment (a reading inventory which focuses on the shapes of the letters and the sounds they make and on rhyming and blending letter sounds) and the TGMD-2 Test of Gross Motor Development (a normative-based assessment that measures locomotor skills and object control skills).

Parent's signature _____

Figure 1.1 Letter to parents explaining the PMLL program.

Stomp boards (A stomp board is a board that has an extra piece on the bottom to boost the back of the board up so it lays at a slant. When a student steps on the raised end of the board whatever is on the front of the board flies into the air to be caught.)

Some activities also use the following equipment, which can be found in equipment catalogues like US Games, Sportime, Palos, Flaghouse, Nasco, or Gopher.

Cup-and-ball sets

Small latex animals (used for tossing, catching, and launching)

Bucket stilts

In addition, many of the activities require plastic mats that you can easily construct from heavy, clear vinyl that is available at most fabric or craft stores and even at discount stores in the craft department. Get the heaviest grade available. You'll also need duct tape in different colors (can also be purchased at fabric, craft, or discount stores). The mats have plastic sleeves to hold the active learning cards underneath the mat and protect them from getting damaged. A cone collar, which is a sleeve with a clear pocket all the way around that fits on top of the cone, can also be used with the active learning cards. These full-color cards, which you can download and print from the web resource, feature shapes, numbers, letters, pictures, and words. They bring an academic component to the activity by calling on students to say what is on a given card while performing a station's indicated movement.

Floor Mat

Figure 1.2 shows you how your finished product should look.

- Cut a piece of plastic to make a rectangular mat that is 3 feet wide by 7 feet long (0.9 by 2.1 meters).
- Place two strips of duct tape (any color you choose) longways on the mat; they should be 12 inches (30 centimeters) apart.
- Place six strips of duct tape across the mat; they should be 12 inches apart.
- To secure the active learning cards, place two pieces of hook-and-loop fastener (e.g., Velcro) on the back of the mat on the top edge of the tape line. Turn the mat over and secure the plastic sleeves with the pockets facing out.

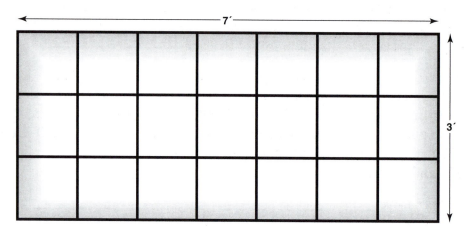

Figure 1.2 Diagram of floor mat.

Hopscotch Mat

- Cut a piece of plastic to 2.5 feet wide by 8 feet long (about 0.8 by 2.4 meters).
- Use duct tape to make 12-inch (30-centimeter) squares down the length of the plastic—three squares in a straight line; two squares side by side; one square aligned with the first three; two squares side by side; one square aligned with the first three (see figure 1.3).
- To secure the active learning cards, place two pieces of hook-and-loop fastener (e.g., Velcro) on the back of the mat on the top edge of the tape line. Turn the mat over and secure the plastic sleeves with the pockets facing out.

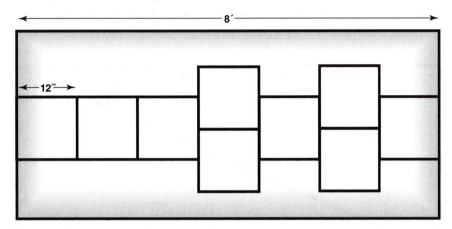

Figure 1.3 Diagram of hopscotch mat.

Ladder Mat

- Cut a piece of plastic to 2.5 feet wide by 8 feet long (0.8 by 2.4 meters).
- Place two 7-foot (2-meter) strips of duct tape (any color you choose) the length of the mat; they should be 12 inches (30 centimeters) apart.
- Beginning 12 inches from the end of the long strips of tape, place six strips of duct tape 12 inches apart to connect the two long pieces of tape and create the rungs of the ladder (see figure 1.4).
- To secure the active learning cards, place two pieces of hook-and-loop fastener (e.g., Velcro) on the back of the mat on the top edge of the tape line. Turn the mat over and secure the plastic sleeves with the pocket facing out.

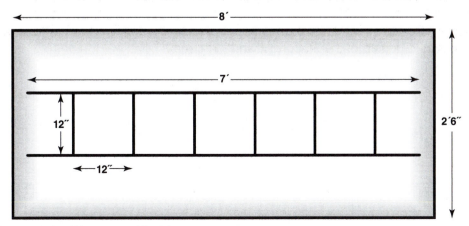

Figure 1.4 Diagram of ladder mat.

Leap, Hop, and Jump Mat

Figure 1.5a shows you the first step in making your leap, hop, and jump mat and figure 1.5b shows you how your finished product should look.

- Cut an 8-foot (2.4-meter) plastic rectangle diagonally as shown in figure 1.5a.
- Place strips of duct tape across the mat; they should be 12 inches (30 centimeters) apart.
- To secure the active learning cards, place two pieces of hook-and-loop fastener (e.g., Velcro) on the back of the mat on the vertical piece of tape on the edge of the tape line. These cards should lay horizontal in between the vertical pieces of tape. Turn the mat over and secure the plastic sleeves with the pocket facing out.

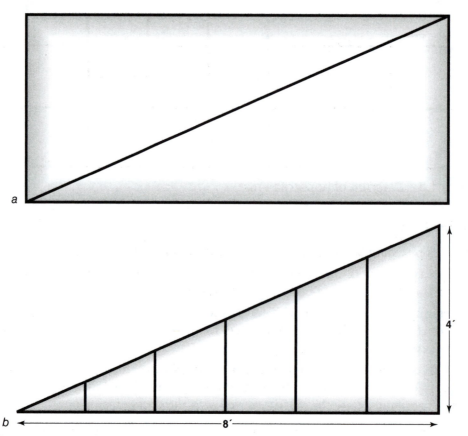

Figure 1.5 *(a)* Cut a rectangular piece of plastic diagonally and *(b)* add tape as shown to construct the leap, hop, and jump mat.

Wall Mat

Figure 1.6 shows you how your finished product should look.

- Cut a piece of plastic to make a rectangle that is 2.5 feet tall by 4 feet wide (0.8 by 1.2 meters).
- Place strips of duct tape (any color you choose) longways on the mat; they should be 12 inches (30 centimeters) apart.
- Place strips of duct tape across the mat; they should be 12 inches apart.
- To secure the active learning cards, place two pieces of hook-and-loop fastener (e.g., Velcro) on the back of the mat on the top edge of the tape line. Turn the mat over and secure the plastic sleeves with the pocket facing out.
- To place the grommets you will need to purchase a grommet tool. These can be found at fabric, craft, or discount stores. You will also need a hammer and a razor blade. Mark the positions of the grommets on the back side of the vinyl by tracing around the inside opening of the eyelet. Cut out the hole or cut an X on the inside of the circle that you traced. Insert the eyelet in the hole and position it on the fabric. Place a washer over the eyelet, with the teeth down. Working on a very hard, protected surface, position the stud end of the tool into the barrel of the eyelet and hammer forcefully.

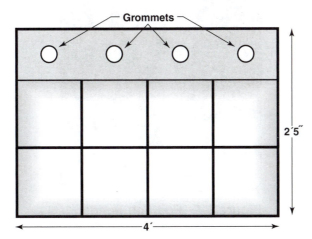

Figure 1.6   Diagram of wall mat.

We use Foo-Foo wands to make learning body awareness and transference fun and nonthreatening. When we call out the name of a body part, they use the wand to point to the body part. In transference we call out a shape, letter, or number and the students trace it in the air with the wand.

Foo-Foo Wands
- Use the cardboard from a wire coat hanger.
- Wrap floor tape (electrical tape) of any color around the cardboard to cover it.
- Fold a handful of silver Christmas tinsel in half and tape the folded end with masking tape so it is thick enough to stay in the end of the cardboard tube.
- Tuck the taped end of the tinsel into the end of the tape-wrapped cardboard (see figure 1.7).

Figure 1.7   Foo-Foo wands.

SCREENING THE STUDENTS

We recommend that you conduct screenings in order to identify students who would benefit from participating in the lab and to establish a baseline for assessing participants' gains. Can you start a PMLL without doing these tests? Absolutely—if you work in a small setting with a small group of students, every student would benefit from the lab, regardless of whether screening is used to document progress. Testing is not essential to run a lab but it is essential for anyone wanting to show improvement and correlate gross motor gains compared to reading gains. A lab can be formed by just taking reading scores or by just testing and taking gross motor scores. Our research is from testing students with the TGMD-2 and correlating them with TPRI scores and we take the lowest of the two scores. These students participate in our lab. This is ideal because we can correlate pre- and post-tests and show tremendous gains to our administration and district heads.

If your student group is large enough that the lab will not accommodate them all, then you will need to select which students to include in the lab. Doing so involves determining which students have the greatest need of participating, which means identifying those who score lowest on motor development screening and cognitive screening.

It is best to include both gross motor and cognitive development in your screening since you want to see improvement in both areas. In a school setting, the academic assessment might be administered by the classroom teacher, and the motor skills assessment might be administered by the physical education teacher. Testing should be performed after the first 3 or 4 weeks of school as this gives the child time to get accustomed to structured classroom schedules and the routines within the environment.

We recommend using the following standardized instruments for determining success: the TGMD-2 Test of Gross Motor Development—Second Edition and the TPRI Early Reading Assessment for academic development. If you work with a sizable Spanish-speaking population, you can use the Tejas LEE test to assess reading skills and academic readiness among students who speak primarily Spanish.

The TPRI (www.tpri.org) serves as a valid and reliable assessment tool that provides a comprehensive picture of a student's reading and language arts development. The test is designed to be used with students in kindergarten through third grade. In the test, a quick screening section works with a more detailed inventory to help teachers identify strengths and problem areas and monitor progress. The TPRI is not the only reading assessment available, but it is the one we have used to conduct screening in our program and to establish the evidence for academic gains among our participants.

The Tejas LEE reading inventory (www.tejaslee.org) is a TPRI equivalent designed for use with Spanish-speaking students. This tool helps teachers quickly assess the early reading skills of students in kindergarten through third grade. The purposes of Tejas LEE are as follows:

- To provide a Spanish reading instrument for school districts
- To detect early reading difficulties or the risk of reading difficulties in Spanish reading at an early level (grades K-3)
- To provide a summary of reading skills and comprehension that teachers can use in planning individual or group instruction

The TGMD-2 (www.proedinc.com) is a norm-referenced measure of common gross motor skills that can be used by kinesiologists, general and special educators, psychologists, and physical therapists. This test helps you identify children (age 3 through age 10 years 11 months) who significantly trail their peers in gross motor skill development. The TGMD-2 addresses 12 skills (6 for each subtest):

- Locomotor: run, gallop, hop, leap, horizontal jump, slide
- Object control: stationary ball strike, stationary dribble, kick, catch, overhand throw, underhand roll

When administering the TGMD-2, it is a good idea if you and a partner each take certain criteria of the test and assess the same criteria every time. This keeps the scoring consistent and makes it easier on the person giving the assessment to be familiar with certain criteria. Again, this is not the only available test of gross motor development, but it is the one we have used in our program. We chose this test because it is a normative based test where students are evaluated based on their age. Most scores improve as the students get older and have to score higher on their post-test to earn the same ratings.

As an alternative to purchasing the TGMD-2 or another motor-skills testing program, you can choose to use a similar gross motor skill assessment provided in the online resource. Simply download the file and save it to your device. You can then create multiple copies (e.g., one for each class or other grouping) and manage students' names and results electronically, if you wish, or you can print as many copies of the assessment as you need and keep them handy on a clipboard during the screening.

As students execute the skills, observe their technique and score them according to predetermined criteria shown in the skill assessment record (see figure 1.8 for a sample). To score the test on the skill assessment record, mark as follows:

C (if you observed the skill component done correctly)

X (if the skill component is not observed or not done correctly)

Skill Assessment Record: Gallop

Name	Arms flexed and move in a pendular motion		Lead foot remains the same		Child faces forward when galloping		Child continues to gallop to the cone and back	

Figure 1.8 Sample page from skill assessment record (full assessment form can be found in the online resource).

Some of the events are not developmentally appropriate for all students. Thus, if a student is unable to complete an event, do not feel concerned. To track progress, simply compare each participant's number of Cs on the pretest with the number of Cs on the post-test.

Set up the screening stations according to the following instructions. Each event should be done twice by each child, to provide an average of skill performance. Also, there are many indicators for each skill and it is difficult to observe them all at one trial.

LOCOMOTOR EVENTS

Locomotor events include walking, running, galloping, hopping, and long jumping.

WALK

Place two cones 20 feet (about 6 meters) apart. Starting behind the first cone, the student walks to and touches the second cone, then walks back to the first cone.

RUN

Place two cones 25 feet (about 7.5 meters) apart. Starting behind the first cone, the student runs to and touches the second cone, then runs back to the first cone.

GALLOP

Place cones 20 feet (about 6 meters) apart. Starting behind the first cone, the student gallops to and touches the second cone, then gallops back to the first cone.

HOP (ON ONE FOOT)

The student hops five times on one foot and then five times on the other. Ensure that the available space is 15 feet (about 4.5 meters) long.

LONG JUMP

From a line on the floor, the child jumps, taking off and landing with both feet.

OBJECT CONTROL EVENTS

Object control events include the underhand toss, catching, kicking, hitting a ball on a tee, and dribbling.

UNDERHAND TOSS

The child tosses a beanbag toward the ceiling to a height slightly above his or her head five times with both hands together. With each toss, the child catches the beanbag with two hands held in a bird's nest style. A bird's nest catch is when both hands are palms up and together side by side, pinkies touching.

CATCH

Use floor tape to place two lines 10 feet (3 meters) apart or use a line that is already provided on the floor (e.g., the lines on a basketball court). The child stands on one line and waits to catch a lightweight, softball-size (4-inch or 10-centimeter) ball tossed from the other line. All criteria is performed twice.

KICK

Use floor tape to place two lines 10 feet (3 meters) apart or use a line that is already provided on the floor (e.g., the lines on a basketball court). The student stands on one line, and a foam soccer ball is placed on the other line. The child runs up from the first line and, without stopping, kicks the ball.

HITTING A BALL ON A TEE

Place a batting tee 8 feet from a wall and facing the wall. (We use a ball tied to the tee with yarn.) Place a lightweight, 4-inch (10-centimeter) ball on the tee at the child's waist height and tell him or her to hit the ball with a plastic bat.

DRIBBLE

With either hand, the child dribbles an 8-inch (20-centimeter) playground ball five times.

BALANCE EVENTS

Balance events assess both dynamic and stationary balance.

DYNAMIC BALANCE

The child walks on a line (use floor tape to place lines or use lines already provided on the floor) with a motion that is either heel to toe or flat on the foot (it is up to the child to decide which). The line should be at least 15 feet (about 4.5 meters) long.

STATIONARY BALANCE

The child should have an area in which to balance (we use a hoop). The child stands on one foot and balances for 8 seconds, then does the same on the other foot. It is helpful to use a stopwatch to time the event.

RUNNING THE LAB

Here is a potpourri of tips that we have gleaned from experience to help you run your lab smoothly.

- Locate each station in the same area every time that students come into the lab. The specific equipment will vary from week to week, but the station placement should never change.

- Assign students to stations so they know exactly where to start every time. The stations should be in sequential order, each featuring a cone cover that tells the student which station to go to next. The rotation should always move in the same order.

- Place students in groups of about four, being certain to take their abilities and personalities into consideration (e.g., if students in the group are aggressive or shy or the level of their abilities differ). All students in each group need to get along in order to succeed. You may need to make several grouping changes in order to find the right combination. Encourage the students to work together and help each other succeed.

- If your group is larger, add more stations; if it is smaller, use fewer stations. We have used eight stations for each week, but this is only a suggestion. If you need to downsize your lab, use fewer stations and pick which ones will most benefit your students for the week. At each station there should be enough equipment for each student to be engaged the whole time unless it is a mat activity, beam activity, or any activity that requires students to take turns on the apparatus (e.g., the jump box with the tumbling wedge or the activity where the students lie on a scooter board and pull themselves with a jump rope).

- You will also need to plan your stations according to the number of adults available to monitor the activity and help students where needed (e.g., an adult needs to be at any station that is off the ground, like the balance beam).

- Station music is a must. Station music is music that plays for a certain amount of time and then pauses automatically and allows the students to switch stations numerically. This is a very important organizational tool that keeps the teacher on time, but most importantly cues students when to stop, clean, and rotate, and when to play. Appropriate tracks are provided in the web resource. You can download these files and burn them to a CD or play them from a mobile device. You can facilitate rotation by using 3-minute recordings interrupted by a 15-second break (to provide time for students to rotate), thus giving participants an auditory cue to move to the next station.

  Become familiar with the stations and any special directions before presenting them to the students. On the first day of the week that you conduct your laboratory, guide your students through each activity, even if they have done them in the past. The next week the stations will change and on the first day of the lab the teacher will explain again. The rest of the days of the lab for that week the students will come in and begin when the music begins. This goes on every week throughout the lab.

- Remind students of safety rules each time they enter the gym. Make certain that you closely monitor all stations at which students are operating above floor level (e.g., jump box, floor beam).

- Be flexible and make changes as necessary to meet your students' needs. Let students be successful by having them do the same stations for the entire week. Immediate success is not guaranteed, but practice will make a big difference.

- You may need to watch different stations each day so that you can give individual help where needed. If it is evident that more practice time is needed, repeat the stations the following week. Remove any stations that appear to be too difficult for most participants. You can always try them again later.

- Give lots of support, encouragement, and praise!

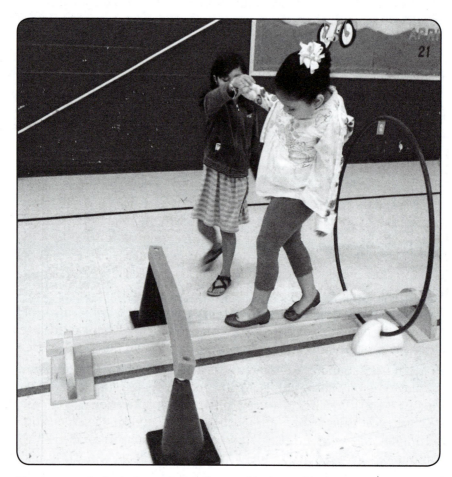

Encourage students to work together and help each other succeed.

ASSESSING PROGRESS

Although informal assessments are not necessary during the course of the PMLL, it's easy to get ongoing informal feedback in the normal course of the lab as you monitor students who are doing the activities.

It is best to repeat the screening process when the lab is complete. As educators, we feel that any improvement constitutes success because a child can only be the best that he or she can be. However, post-testing should be done in order to document the success of the program. Results from the assessment should be shared with your administration in order to support your program. Some students may not have fully developed cognitively according to the TPRI even though their scores have gone up, and this outcome does constitute success. The program was designed for general education students, but is very beneficial to special education students as well.

Figure 1.9 shows our lab students' gains in *(a)* gross motor and *(b)* reading scores as compared to a control group. These are the results that have demonstrated to our administration and parents that the program really works!

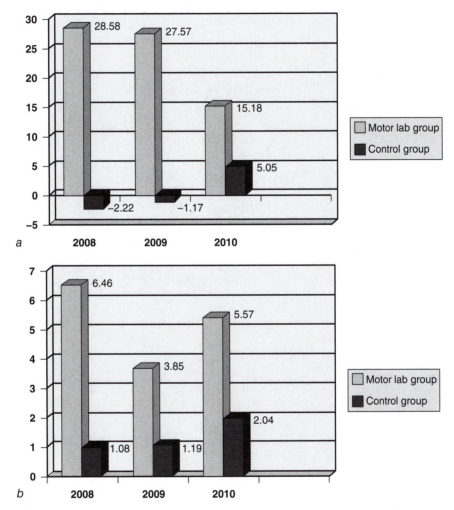

Figure 1.9 These graphs compare the gains in *(a,* as measured by the TGMD-2) gross motor test scores and *(b,* as measured by the TPRI) reading test scores of students who took part in the perceptual-motor learning laboratory and a control group who did not participate in the lab. The graphs represent testing over three years (2008-2010).

SUMMARY

All children should be given the opportunity to develop the perceptual-motor skills needed to enhance and support the development of the intellectual skills that result in academic and life success. As educators, our job is to ensure that every student can achieve and be the best that he or she can be. The practice of moving, learning, and having fun while developing the neural pathways in a child's brain is easy, logical, and extremely gratifying.

2

BILATERAL ACTIVITIES

Bilateral movement activities develop motor control and coordination. If a child does not master bilateral movements, his or her learning and cognitive development are negatively affected due to the lack of neural stimulations that promote organization of the brain. Poor coordination of the left and right sides of the body by the brain results in disintegration of function.

Use the following guide to choosing the appropriate active learning cards for each week:

Week 1: Colors and shapes

Week 2: Numbers

Week 3: Lowercase letters

Week 4: Lowercase letters with pictures

Week 5: Uppercase letters

Week 6: Uppercase letters with pictures

Week 7: Lowercase letters and spelling words

Week 8: Uppercase letters and spelling words

Although these categories give you general guidelines to go by, some specific activities might call for a different category than described here.

Skills Developed

Laterality, locomotor skills, motor planning

Equipment

- Six cones with clear sleeves
- Active learning cards (shapes)

Setup

Place six cones approximately 4 feet (1.2 meters) apart in a straight line. (The photo shows a variant setup in which cones are staggered.) Each cone's sleeve should contain an active learning card showing a colored shape.

Activity

Facing forward, jump from cone to cone. Take off and land with both feet. Along the way, touch the top of each cone with both hands at the same time and say the shape and color shown on the card for that cone.

Skill Check

- Make sure that the students jump from cone to cone rather than run.
- Remind the student to slow down and focus on using the correct form for a standing long jump:
    - Bend both knees with your arms extended behind your body before takeoff.
    - When jumping, thrust your arms forcefully forward and upward (above your head).
    - Take off and land with both feet.
    - Move your arms downward on landing.

Skills Developed

Laterality, locomotor skills, motor planning

Equipment

- Hopscotch mat
- Active learning cards (shapes)

Activity

Jump with both feet from square to square. On landing, say the shape and color shown on the card for the square you land in.

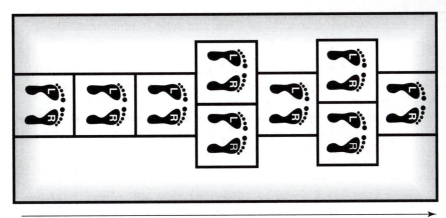

Jump in each square

Skill Check

- The student may try to do a traditional hopscotch pattern. Make sure that he or she jumps with both feet simultaneously into each square.
- Remind the student to slow down and focus on using the correct form for a standing long jump:
  - Bend both knees with your arms extended behind your body before takeoff.
  - When jumping, thrust your arms forcefully forward and upward (above your head).
  - Take off and land with both feet.
  - Move your arms downward on landing.

Skills Developed

Laterality, locomotor skills, motor planning

Equipment

- Floor mat
- Wall mat
- Active learning cards (shapes)

Setup

- The suction hooks of the wall mat should be attached to the wall four feet from the floor.
- If you make two sets of the cards, you may use the same card in adjacent squares. If you only have one set of cards, go ahead and put different cards in each square.

Activity

- Floor mat: Jump with both feet at the same time. Your feet should land side by side with each foot in its own square. On landing, say the color and shape on the cards for both squares you land in.

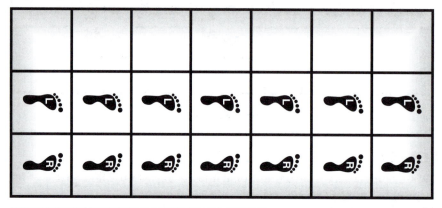

- Wall mat: Place your hands in adjacent squares of the wall mat at the same time. While touching the squares, say the color and shape shown on the card for each square. Move on to the next pair of squares.

Skill Check

- The student should speak loudly in saying what is shown on the cards.
- Ensure that the student touches both hands to the wall mat at the same time.
- Remind the student to slow down and focus on using the correct form for a standing long jump:
  - Bend both knees with your arms extended behind your body before takeoff.
  - When jumping, thrust your arms forcefully forward and upward (above your head).
  - Take off and land with both feet.
  - Move your arms downward on landing.

Skills Developed

Laterality, dynamic balance

Equipment

- Floor beam—best if about 6 feet (2 meters) long and no more than 6 inches (15 centimeters) off the floor
- 8.5-inch (22-centimeter) playground ball
- Active learning cards (shapes)

Setup

Place eight active learning cards along the beam—four cards on either side (with the cards on each side spaced 2 feet or about half a meter apart from each other).

Activity

1. Face the front of the balance beam and walk forward while holding the ball with both hands.
2. Walk backward on the beam while holding the ball with both hands.
3. When walking forward, bounce the ball on the cards on the right side. When walking backward, bounce the ball on the cards on the left side.

Skill Check

- Remind the student to hold the ball in both hands (some will try to carry it with one hand).
- Remind the student not to hurry but to establish good balance before taking each step.
- If a student experiences severe difficulty on the beam, allow him or her to walk on a line on the floor.
- Make sure that the student uses proper form for dribbling:
  - Keep your eyes up.
  - Use your finger pads—not your fingertips.
  - For good control, dribble at your side and at waist level or lower.
  - Dribble the ball in your "foot pocket" created by dropping your right foot behind your left foot (or vice versa if using left hand).
- Make sure that the student uses proper form for walking:
  - Stand tall by keeping your body erect.
  - You should be able to draw a straight line from ear to shoulder.
  - Align your hips, knees, and ankles.
  - Your head should be level and looking forward, and your chin should be parallel to the ground.
  - Your shoulders should be relaxed and your arms bent.
  - Swing your arms in opposition to your foot movement.
  - Walk heel to toe.

Skills Developed

Motor planning, gross motor coordination

Equipment

- Ladder mat
- Active learning cards (shapes)

Activity

Jump over each rung of the ladder with both feet at the same time. On landing, say the color and shape shown on the card for the square you jumped into.

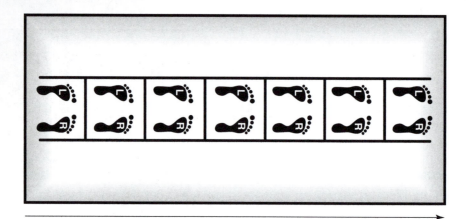

Skill Check

- Remind the student to speak loudly when saying the shapes and colors as he or she jumps.
- Remind the student to slow down and focus on using the correct form for a standing long jump:
  - Bend both knees with your arms extended behind your body before takeoff.
  - When jumping, thrust your arms forcefully forward and upward (above your head).
  - Take off and land with both feet.
  - Move your arms downward on landing.

Skills Developed

Spatial awareness, eye–hand coordination

Equipment

- One hoop for each child in colors coordinated with those of the shapes if possible—size optional but 30-inch (1-meter) recommended
- One 8.5-inch (22-centimeter) playground ball for each child
- Active learning cards (shapes)

Setup

Place the hula hoops in a straight line 3 feet (about 1 meter) apart. Put an active learning card inside each hoop.

Activity

1. Walk around the outside of the first hoop while bouncing the ball inside of the hoop with both hands.
2. While bouncing the ball, say the color and shape shown on the card inside the circle.
3. Move from hoop to hoop and repeat with all of the hoops.

Skill Check

- The student should bounce the ball with the fingertips (no slapping).
- The ball should contact the surface in front of the student.
- The student should maintain control of the ball for at least four consecutive bounces.

Skills Developed

Laterality, motor planning, gross motor coordination

Equipment

Poly spots (different colors)

Setup

Place 6 poly spots in a straight line 1 foot (about 0.3 meters) apart.

Activity

Frog-jump from poly spot to poly spot. When you land on each poly spot, say the color of the spot.

Skill Check

Remind the student to slow down and focus on using the correct form for a frog jump.

- Start in a squat position.
- Place your hands on the floor between your legs.
- Move your hands to a position on the floor a short distance in front of your body.
- Keeping your feet together and your hands on the floor, jump and let your feet land near your hands.

Skills Developed

Body awareness, motor planning, gross motor coordination

Equipment

None

Activity

1. Do five straddle jumps (jumping jacks with feet only). After each jump, say the first five letters of the alphabet.
2. Do five jumping jacks with only the arm movement. Repeat the first five letters of the alphabet after each movement.
3. Do five slow jumping jacks (arms and legs), counting each jump out loud.

Skill Check

Remind students to slow down and focus on using the correct form for jumping jacks:

- Start by standing with your feet together and your arms at your sides. Jump so that your feet are shoulder-width apart and your hands are together above your head (move hands and feet at the same time).
- Jump again, bringing your feet back together and your arms back to your sides in the original position.

Skills Developed

Locomotor skills, motor planning, spatial awareness

Equipment

- Ten cones with clear sleeves
- Active learning cards (numbers 1–10)

Setup

Scatter the cones 4 feet (1.2 meters) apart as shown in the diagram.

Activity

Frog-jump randomly from cone to cone. When you get to each cone, touch it and say the color and number shown on its card. (This activity is the same as the one for station 1 in week 3 except that it uses a different number of cones.)

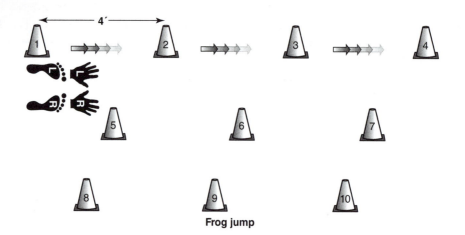

Frog jump

Skill Check

Remind the student to slow down and focus on using the correct form for a frog jump.

- Start in a squat position.
- Place your hands on the floor between your legs.
- Move your hands to a position on the floor a short distance in front of your body.
- Keeping your feet together and your hands on the floor, jump and let your feet land near your hands.

Skills Developed

Laterality, locomotor skills, motor planning

Equipment

- Hopscotch mat
- Active learning cards (numbers)

Activity

Jump with both feet from square to square, bouncing two times in each square. On landing, say the color and number shown on the card for that square.

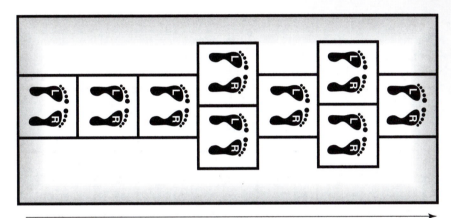

Jump 2 times in each square

Skill Check

- The student may try to do a traditional hopscotch pattern. Make sure that he or she jumps with both feet simultaneously into each square.
- Remind the student to slow down and focus on using the correct form for a standing long jump:
  - Bend both knees with your arms extended behind your body before takeoff.
  - Thrust your arms forcefully forward and upward (above your head) when jumping.
  - Take off and land with both feet.
  - Move your arms downward on landing.

Skills Developed

Laterality, motor planning, gross motor coordination

Equipment

- Floor mat
- Wall mat
- Active learning cards (numbers)

Setup

If you make two sets of the cards, you may use the same card in adjacent squares. If you only have one set of cards, go ahead and put different cards in each square.

Activity

- Floor mat: Jump with both feet at the same time. Your feet should land side by side with each foot in its own square. When landing, say the color and shape on the cards for both squares you land in. (This activity is the same as the one for week 1, station 3.)

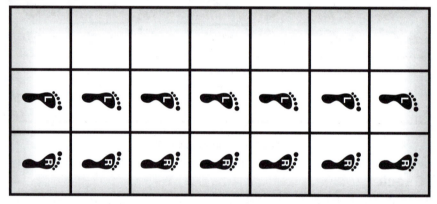

- Wall mat: Jump one time in front of the mat and tap the mat once with both hands at the same time in adjacent squares. Say the color and number shown on each card as you tap it. Move on to the next pair of squares.

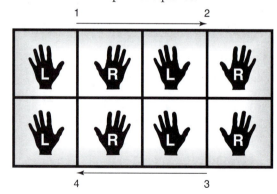

Skill Check

- The student should speak loudly in saying what is shown on the cards.
- Ensure that the student touches both hands to the wall mat at the same time.
- Remind the student to focus on using the correct form for a standing long jump:
  - Bend both knees with your arms extended behind your body before takeoff.
  - When jumping, thrust your arms forcefully forward and upward (above your head).
  - Take off and land with both feet.
  - Move your arms downward on landing.

Skills Developed

Locomotor skills, motor planning, spatial awareness

Equipment

Foo-Foo wands (two per student)

Activity

1. Touch your toes with your wands (touch one wand to each foot) and say "toes."
2. Touch your knees with your wands and say "knees."
3. Touch your shoulders with your wands and say "shoulders."
4. Touch your head with both wands and say "head."

Skill Check

Make sure that the student uses the Foo-Foo wands properly. Students tend to use the Foo-Foo wands as swords or objects to hit each other with. Wands are to be used specifically to identify body parts.

Skills Developed

Motor planning, gross motor coordination, spatial awareness

Equipment

- Ladder mat
- Active learning cards (shapes)

Activity

Jump through the ladder one square a time by doing jumping jacks—two feet in the first square, two feet out of the second square (one foot to either side), two feet in the third square, and so on. Say the color and shape shown for each square as you land in it.

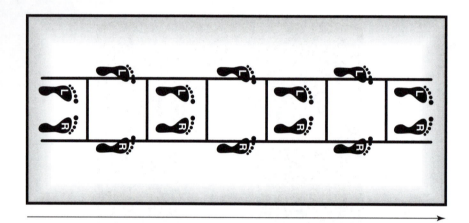

Skill Check

- Encourage the student to slow down and say what is shown on the cards.
- Remind the student to slow down and focus on using the correct form for jumping jacks:
  - Start by standing with your feet together and your arms at your sides. Jump so that your feet are shoulder-width apart and your hands are together above your head (move hands and feet at the same time).
  - Jump again, bringing your feet back together and your arms back to your sides in the original position.

Skills Developed

Laterality, motor planning, gross motor coordination

Equipment

- One stomp board for each child
- One beanbag for each child

Activity

1. Stomp on the stomp board with both feet at once to project the beanbag into the air. Catch the beanbag with two hands and say the color of the beanbag. Try five times.

2. Stomp on the stomp board with both feet at once to project the beanbag into the air. Clap once and catch the beanbag with two hands. Try five times.

Skill Check

- Make sure that the student uses both feet while stomping.
- Remind the student to slow down and focus on using the correct form for a bird's nest catch (two-hand catch with palms up):
  - Prepare by extending your hands in front of your body with your elbows bent.
  - Reach for the beanbag with your palms up as the beanbag approaches.
  - Catch the beanbag with your hands only—not against your chest.
  - Keep your eyes on the beanbag while catching it.

Skills Developed

Spatial awareness, gross motor coordination

Equipment

- Eight hoops (28-30 inches in diameter; the color of the hoop should match that of the active learning card)
- One 8.5-inch (22-centimeter) playground ball for each child
- Active learning cards (shapes)

Setup

Place hoops in a circle 3 feet (about 1 meter) apart. Put an active learning card inside each hoop.

Activity

Starting at the first hoop, say the shape and color shown on the card in the hoop. Then use a two-handed dribble to dribble the ball in the hoop five times, counting from 1 to 5 as you dribble. Move to the next hoop and repeat.

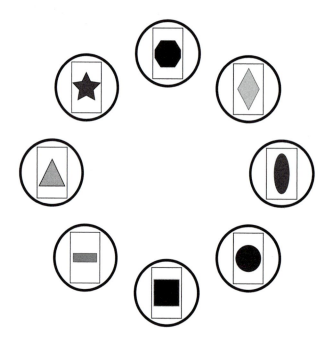

Skill Check

- The ball should contact the surface in front of the student.
- Keep your eyes up.
- Use your finger pads—not your fingertips.
- For good control, dribble at waist level or lower.
- The student should maintain control of the ball for at least four consecutive bounces.

Skills Developed

Eye–hand coordination, tracking skills

Equipment

- One beanbag for each student
- Six cones
- Active learning cards (numbers)

Setup

Place six cones in a straight line approximately 4 feet (1.2 meters) apart with the learning cards in numerical order.

Activity

Jump from cone to cone and toss and catch the beanbag five times with both hands while identifying numbers and colors.

Skill Check

Make sure that the student uses a bird's nest catch.

- Prepare by extending your hands in front of your body with your elbows bent.
- Reach for the beanbag with your palms up as the beanbag approaches.
- Catch the beanbag with your hands only—not against your chest.
- Keep your eyes on the beanbag while catching it.

Skills Developed

Locomotor skills, motor planning, spatial awareness

Equipment

- Ten cones with clear sleeves
- Active learning cards (numbers)

Setup

The cones should be scattered 4 feet (1.2 meters) apart throughout the space.

Activity

Bunny-hop from cone to cone. When you get to a cone, touch it and say the color and number shown on it. (This activity is the same as the one for week 2, station 1 except that it uses a bunny hop instead of a frog jump.) To extend this lesson as the week progresses, you can change the numbers to offer whatever challenge you think is appropriate for the students.

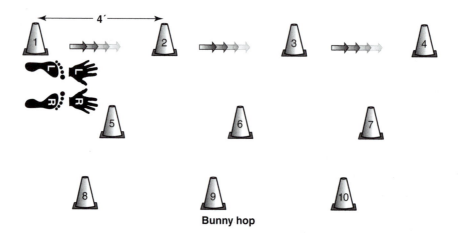

Bunny hop

Skill Check

Remind the student to slow down and focus on using the correct form for a bunny hop:

- Start in a squat position.
- Place your hands on the floor between your legs.
- Move your hands to a position on the floor a short distance in front of your body.
- Keeping your feet together, jump up and land back in a squat position with your hands on the floor between your legs.

Skills Developed

Laterality, locomotor skills, motor planning

Equipment

- Hopscotch mat
- Active learning cards (numbers)

Activity

Jump backward from square to square with both feet together. On each landing in each square, say the number and color shown on the card for that square.

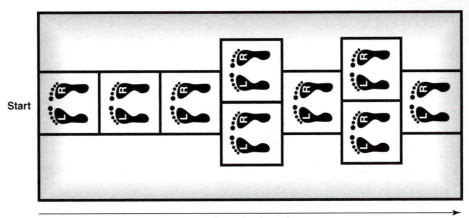

Start

Jump backward

Skill Check

- The student may try to do a traditional hopscotch pattern—make sure that he or she jumps and lands with both feet in each square,
- Make sure that the student uses correct jumping form:
  - Bend both knees with your arms extended behind your body before takeoff.
  - When jumping, thrust your arms forcefully forward and upward (above your head).
  - Take off and land with both feet.
  - Move your arms downward on landing.

Skills Developed

Laterality, motor planning, gross motor coordination

Equipment

- Floor mat
- Wall mat
- Active learning cards (numbers)
- Stick-on hooks

Setup

Use stick-on hooks to attach the mat to the wall.

Activity

- Floor mat: Jump through the mat with both feet at the same time. Your feet should land side by side with each foot in its own square. On each landing, clap your hands.

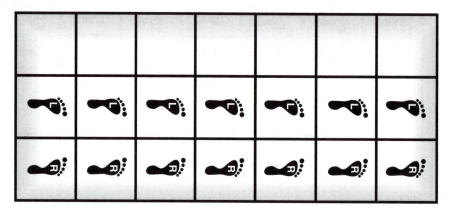

- Wall mat: Jump twice in front of the mat and touch the mat with both hands at the same time in adjacent squares. Say the color and number shown on each card as you hit it. Move on to the next pair of squares.

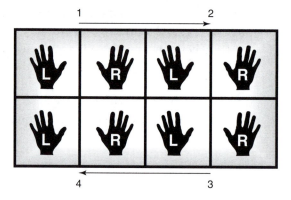

Skill Check

- Encourage the student to say aloud the number and color on the card.
- Ensure that the student hits the wall mat squares with both hands at the same time.
- Remind the student to focus on using the correct form for a standing long jump:
    - Bend both knees with your arms extended behind your body before takeoff.
    - When jumping, thrust your arms forcefully forward and upward (above your head).
    - Take off and land with both feet.
    - Move your arms downward on landing.

Skills Developed

Directionality, motor planning, gross motor coordination

Equipment

One hoop for each child

Activity

1. Begin with both feet in the first hoop.
2. Jump from hoop to hoop, making a quarter-turn with each jump.
3. Work your way through the letters of the alphabet after each jump.

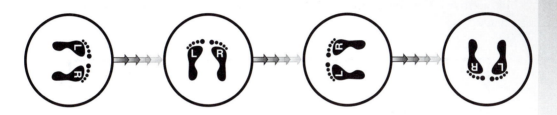

Skill Check

Remind students to slow down and focus on using the correct form for a standing long jump:

- Bend both knees with your arms extended behind your body before takeoff.
- When jumping, thrust your arms forcefully forward and upward (above your head).
- Take off and land with both feet.
- Move your arms downward on landing.

Skills Developed

Motor planning, gross motor coordination, spatial awareness

Equipment

- Ladder mat
- Active learning cards (numbers)

Activity

Jump through the ladder one square a time by doing jumping jacks—two feet in the first square, two feet out of the second square (one foot to either side), two feet in the third square, and so on. Say the color and number shown for each square as you land in it. (This activity is the same as the one for week 2, station 5, but uses number cards instead of shape cards.)

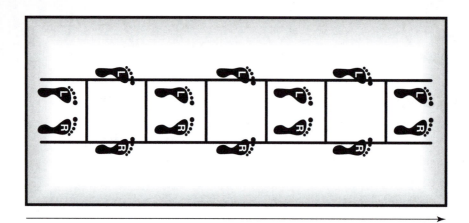

Skill Check

- Encourage the student to slow down and say what is shown on the cards.
- Remind the student to slow down and focus on using the correct form for jumping jacks:
  - Start by standing with your feet together and your arms at your sides.
  - Jump so that your feet are shoulder-width apart and your hands are together above your head (move hands and feet at the same time).
  - Jump again, bringing your feet back together and your arms back to your sides in the original position.

Skills Developed

Motor planning, eye–hand coordination, eye–foot coordination

Equipment

- One stomp board for each child
- One beanbag for each child

Activity

1. Stomp on the stomp board with both feet at once to project the beanbag into the air. Catch the beanbag with two hands while saying the letters of the alphabet. Do five tries.
2. Stomp with both feet to project the beanbag into the air. Clap once and catch the beanbag with two hands while saying the letters of the alphabet. Do five tries.
3. Stomp with both feet to project the beanbag into the air. Hold a paddle with two hands and keep the beanbag in the air with as many paddle hits as possible. Say a letter of the alphabet after each hit.

Skill Check

- Make sure that the student uses both feet while stomping.
- Remind the student to slow down and focus on using the correct form for a bird's nest catch (two-hand catch with palms up):
  - Prepare by extending your hands in front of your body with your elbows bent.
  - Reach for the beanbag with your palms up as the beanbag approaches.
  - Catch the beanbag with your hands only—not against your chest.
  - Keep your eyes on the beanbag while catching it.

Skills Developed

Laterality, motor planning, gross motor coordination

Equipment

- Scooter board
- Rope (6 feet or 2 meters long)
- Volleyball standard or similar apparatus

Setup

Attach the rope to the base of the volleyball standard or similar apparatus and lay it (fully extended) on the floor. Position the scooter at the free end of the rope.

Activity

Lie with your tummy on the scooter board. Grab the rope with both hands at the same place, rather than alternating hands, and pull yourself forward along the rope. Count aloud each time you take a new grip on the rope. How many pulls does it take to reach the end?

Skill Check

- Stress scooter board safety (e.g., never stand on the board, keep hands on the rope, keep hair and clothing away from the wheels).
- The student should stay on his or her tummy.
- The student should use both hands simultaneously.

Skills Developed

Eye–hand coordination, throwing accuracy

Equipment

- 8.5-inch (22-centimeter) playground ball
- Large trash can
- Floor tape

Setup

Use the tape to mark a line on the floor 4 feet (1.2 meters) from the trash can. Students will stand at this line to toss and bounce the ball.

Activity

1. Using both hands, toss the ball into the trash can with an underhand toss and then retrieve the ball. Count each toss. You may skip-count by 2s, 5s, or 10s. Repeat until you have thrown the ball 10 times.

2. Bounce the ball into the trash can with two hands and then retrieve the ball. Start at the beginning of the alphabet and, after each toss, say a letter. Repeat until you have bounced the ball 10 times.

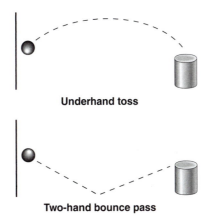

Underhand toss

Two-hand bounce pass

Skill Check

Make sure the student uses both hands to toss and bounce the ball. Their palms should be up and the toss should not be higher than the arms can reach above the head.

Skills Developed

Locomotor skills, motor planning, spatial awareness

Equipment

- Six cones with clear sleeves
- Active learning cards (lowercase letters with pictures)

Setup

Place six cones 4 feet (1.2 meters) apart in a straight line. Place matching letter and picture cards in the cones, alternating with each cone: letter A, apple picture, letter B, ball picture, letter C, cat picture.

Activity

Facing forward, jump from cone to cone. At each cone, say the letter or picture shown on the card for that cone.

Skill Check

- Make sure that the student jumps from cone to cone rather than running.
- Remind the student to slow down and focus on using the correct form for a standing long jump:
  - Bend both knees with your arms extended behind your body before takeoff.
  - When jumping, thrust your arms forcefully forward and upward (above your head).
  - Take off and land on both feet at the same time.
  - Move your arms downward on landing.

Skills Developed

Locomotor skills, motor planning, spatial awareness

Equipment

- Hopscotch mat
- Active learning cards (lowercase letters with pictures)

Activity

Jump with two feet from square to square, making a quarter-turn with each jump. On landing, say the letter and picture shown on the card for the square you are jumping into.

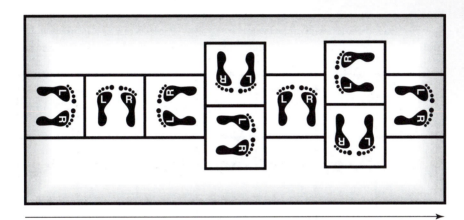

Skill Check

- The student may try to do a traditional hopscotch pattern. Make sure that he or she jumps with both feet simultaneously into each square.
- Remind students to slow down and focus on using the correct form for a standing long jump:
  - Bend both knees with your arms extended behind your body before takeoff.
  - When jumping, thrust your arms forcefully forward and upward (above your head).
  - Take off and land with both feet.
  - Move your arms downward on landing.
  - Make sure the student does a quarter-turn with each jump.

Skills Developed

Laterality, motor planning, gross motor coordination

Equipment

- Floor mat
- Wall mat
- Active learning cards (lowercase letters with pictures)

Setup

If you make two sets of the cards, you may use the same card in adjacent squares. If you only have one set of cards, go ahead and put different cards in each square.

Activity

- Floor mat: Jump with both feet from square to square with your feet landing in adjacent squares each time. Jump twice in each pair of squares. On landing the second time, say the letter and picture shown on the cards for the squares you are in.

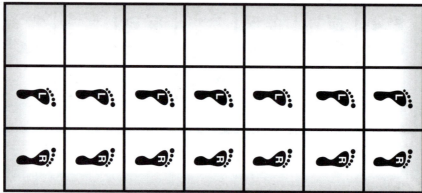

Jump 2 times in each square

- Wall mat: Each time you hit one of the cards with your hands, say the letter and picture shown on the card. To start, stand facing the mat and point your toes diagonally toward the top right corner of the mat. Jump up and hit the top right card with two hands. Next, point your toes toward the middle of the mat and jump up and hit each of the two middle cards with two hands (first one card, then the other). Now, point your toes diagonally toward the top left corner of the mat. Jump up and hit the card with two hands. Repeat the pattern with the cards in the bottom row.

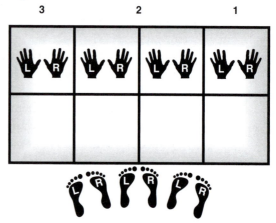

Skill Check

- Encourage the student to say aloud what is shown on the card.
- Watch for correct foot placement.
- Ensure that the student hits the wall mat squares with both hands at the same time.
- Remind the student to focus on using the correct form for a standing long jump:
  - Bend both knees with your arms extended behind your body before takeoff.
  - When jumping, thrust your arms forcefully forward and upward (above your head).
  - Take off and land with both feet.
  - Move your arms downward on landing.

Skills Developed

Directionality, motor planning, gross motor coordination

Equipment

Jump rope

Activity

1. Put the rope on the floor and jump over it from side to side (like a skier). After each jump, say a number (skip-counting by two). Jump in sets of 10. Rest after each set. Skip-count to 20.

2. Put the rope on the floor and jump over it from front to back (like a bell). After each jump, say a number (skip-counting by two). Skip-count to 20. Jump in sets of 10. Rest after each set.

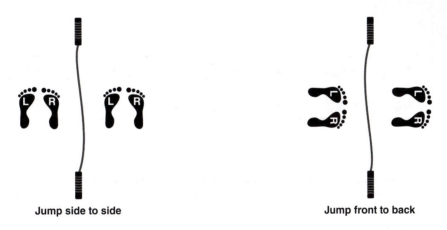

Jump side to side   **Jump front to back**

Skill Check

- Make sure the student keeps the rope on the floor.
- Encourage the student to skip-count by twos.
- Make sure the student uses the proper form for jumping:
  - Bend both knees with your arms extended behind your body before takeoff.
  - When jumping, thrust your arms forcefully forward and upward (above your head).
  - Take off and land with both feet.
  - Move your arms downward on landing.

Skills Developed

Motor planning, gross motor coordination

Equipment

- Ladder mat
- Active learning cards (lowercase letters with pictures)

Activity

While saying what is shown on the active learning cards, jump through the mat. Start at the beginning of the ladder mat facing forward. Jump forward from square to square identifying the letter and picture in each square upon landing.

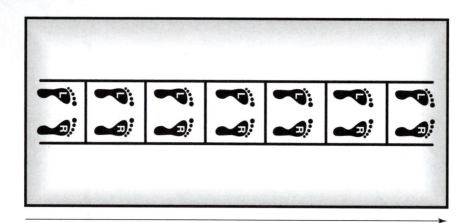

Skill Check

- Encourage the student to speak loudly when saying what is shown on the cards.
- Make sure the student jumps with as little knee bend as possible.
- Emphasize correct jumping form.
  - Bend both knees with your arms extended behind your body before takeoff.
  - When jumping, thrust your arms forcefully forward and upward (above your head).
  - Take off and land with both feet.
  - Move your arms downward on landing.

Skills Developed

Motor planning, eye–hand coordination, eye–foot coordination

Equipment

- One stomp board for each student
- Two beanbags for each student

Activity

1. Stomp on the stomp board with both feet to project the beanbag into the air. Slap your knee once and catch the beanbag with two hands. Repeat until you have tried to catch the beanbag five times.

2. Stomp on the stomp board with both feet to project the beanbag into the air. Clap once and catch the beanbag with two hands. Repeat until you have tried to catch the beanbag five times.

3. Stomp on the stomp board with both feet to project two beanbags into the air. Repeat until you have launched the beanbags five times.

Skill Check

- Make sure that the student uses both feet while stomping.
- Remind the student to slow down and focus on using the correct form for a bird's nest catch (two-hand with palms up).
  - Prepare by extending your hands in front of your body with your elbows bent.
  - Reach for the beanbag with your palms up as the beanbag approaches.
  - Catch the beanbag with your hands only—not against your chest.
  - Keep your eyes on the beanbag while catching it.

Skills Developed

Balance

Equipment

Balance board

Activity

1. Stand on the balance board, holding hands with a partner who is on the floor in front of the board to help you balance. Try to keep the ends of the board off of the floor. Skip-count by twos to 20 and then switch positions with your partner.

2. Try to stand on the board and keep the ends off of the floor without the help of a partner. Skip-count by twos to 20.

Skill Check

Make sure the student uses the correct form for static balance:

- Chin should be parallel to the floor and the feet should not move.
- Arms may be extended outward to facilitate balance.
- The balance pose should be held for a minimum of five seconds.

Skills Developed

Locomotor skills, motor planning, spatial awareness

Equipment

Five noodles

Setup

Place five noodles in a straight line 4 feet (1.2 meters) apart.

Activity

1. Jump over the noodles, taking off and landing with both feet. Each time you jump, say a letter of the alphabet starting at the beginning. Continue in alphabetical order and see how many times you can say the whole alphabet in three minutes.

2. Jump over the noodles slowly with hands on hips and say one letter each time you land. Then jump over the noodles again using quick jumps with hands on hips. Say one letter each time you land.

3. Jump high over the noodles, saying a letter of the alphabet each time you land. Then jump low over the noodles again and say a letter each time you land.

Skill Check

Remind the student to slow down and focus on using the correct form for a standing long jump:

• Bend both knees with your arms extended behind your body before takeoff.
• When jumping, thrust your arms forcefully forward and upward (above your head).
• Take off and land with both feet.
• Move your arms downward on landing.

Skill Developed

Locomotor skills, motor planning, spatial awareness

Equipment

- Six cones with clear sleeves
- Active learning cards (uppercase letters and pictures)

Setup

Place six cones 3 feet (1 meter) apart in a straight line. Place matching letter and picture cards in cones, alternating with each cone: letter A, apple picture, letter B, ball picture, letter C, cat picture.

Activity

Jump sideways from cone to cone. At each cone, touch the cone and say the color and the letter or picture shown on the card.

Skill Check

- Make sure that the student jumps from cone to cone rather than running.
- Remind the student to slow down and focus on using the correct form for sideways jumping:
  - Make sure feet are parallel to each other with toes pointing forward.
  - When jumping, thrust your arms forcefully forward and upward (above your head).
  - Take off and land with both feet.
  - Move your arms downward on landing.

Skills Developed

Laterality, locomotor skills, motor planning

Equipment

- Hopscotch mat
- Active learning cards (uppercase letters)

Activity

Jump with both feet from square to square. On each landing, say what is shown on the card for the square you are jumping into. After each jump, clap your hands twice.

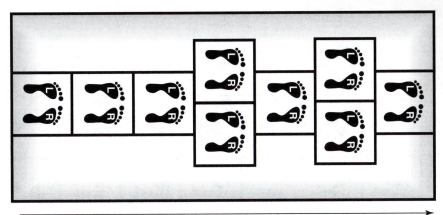

Clap 2 times after each jump

Skill Check

- The student may try to do a traditional hopscotch pattern. Make sure that he or she jumps with both feet simultaneously into each square.
- Remind the student to slow down and focus on using the correct form for a standing long jump:
  - Bend both knees with your arms extended behind your body before takeoff.
  - When jumping, thrust your arms forcefully forward and upward (above your head).
  - Take off and land with both feet.
  - Move your arms downward on landing.

Skills Developed

Laterality, locomotor skills, motor planning

Equipment

- Floor mat
- Wall mat
- Active learning cards (uppercase letters)

Setup

If there are two sets of letters, you may put the same letter in each side by side square. If not, different letters are acceptable.

Activity

- Floor mat: Double-jump backward and continue to the end of the floor mat. Jump with both feet at the same time. Your feet should land side by side with each foot in its own square. On each landing, say the uppercase letters shown on the cards for each square you land in.

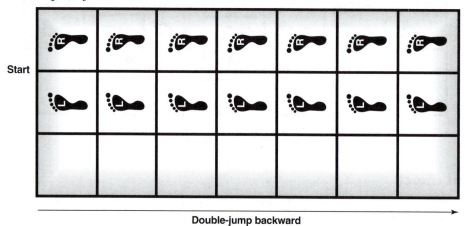

Double-jump backward

- Wall mat: Starting with the top left square of the mat, put your hands on the mat with each hand turned inward. Say what is shown on the card. Move to the next square and turn your hands outward. Say what is shown on the card. Alternate your hands inward and outward, saying what is shown on the current card, as you work

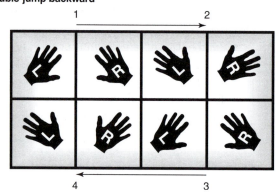

across the mat. When you reach the end of the top row, move down to the bottom row and work back across the mat to the left.

Skill Check

Remind the student to focus on using the correct form for a standing long jump:

- Bend both knees with your arms extended behind your body before takeoff.
- When jumping, thrust your arms forcefully forward and upward (above your head).
- Take off and land with both feet.
- Move your arms downward on landing.

Skills Developed

Laterality, locomotor skills, motor planning

Equipment

- Leap, hop, and jump mat
- Active learning cards (uppercase letters)

Activity

Start at the pointed end of the mat (where the lower number is located). Jump across this first section of the mat with both feet and say the number shown on the card for that section. Move to the next section to the right (with the card for the next higher number) and jump across this section while saying the number shown on the card. Jump over the remaining sections in this way until you reach the end of the mat. You do not need to be able to jump each distance. Jump the longest distance that you are most comfortable with.

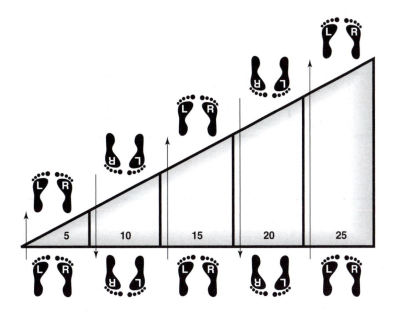

Skill Check

- Encourage the student to speak loudly when saying the numbers as he or she jumps.
- Remind the student to slow down and focus on using the correct form for a standing long jump:
  - Bend both knees with your arms extended behind your body before takeoff.
  - When jumping, thrust your arms forcefully forward and upward (above your head).
  - Take off and land with both feet.
  - Move your arms downward on landing.

Skills Developed

Motor planning, gross motor coordination, locomotor skills

Equipment

- Ladder mat
- Active learning cards (uppercase letters)

Activity

Jump over each rung with both feet at the same time. Follow this pattern: Jump forward three squares, then backward one square. Repeat this process until you reach the end of the ladder. On each landing, say the uppercase letter shown on the card for the square you land in.

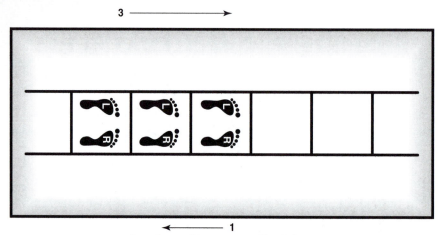

Jump forward 3 squares and back 1 square

Skill Check

- Make sure the student jumps forward three squares and back one square.
- Encourage the student to say aloud what is shown on the cards.
- Remind the student to slow down and focus on using the correct form for a standing long jump:
  - Bend both knees with your arms extended behind your body before takeoff.
  - When jumping, thrust your arms forcefully forward and upward (above your head).
  - Take off and land with both feet.
  - Move your arms downward on landing.

Skills Developed

Motor planning, gross motor coordination, locomotor skills

Equipment

Ten poly spots

Setup

Scatter poly spots on the floor approximately 12 inches (30 centimeters) apart as shown in the diagram.

Activity

1. Do frog jumps from poly spot to poly spot. After each jump and starting with A, work your way through the alphabet. Start over again if you get to the end of the alphabet.

2. Jump sideways through the series of poly spots saying letters in alphabetical order, starting with A, after each jump. Start over again if you get to the end of the alphabet.

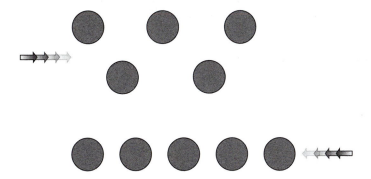

Skill Check

- During sideways jumping, make sure that the student jumps with his or her feet facing forward.
- Remind the student to slow down and focus on using the correct form for a frog jump:
  - Start in a squat position.
  - Place your hands on the floor between your legs.
  - Move your hands to a position on the floor a short distance in front of your body.
  - Keeping your feet together and your hands on the floor, jump and let your feet land near your hands.

Skills Developed

Eye–hand coordination, tracking skills

Equipment

- One 8.5-inch (22-centimeter) playground ball for each child
- Floor tape

Setup

Use floor tape to mark out a line parallel to a wall at a distance of 6 feet (2 meters).

Activity

1. Sit facing the wall and roll the ball to the wall with two hands. After each roll, say the alphabet. Roll as many times as possible in the allotted time.
2. Stand on the line and toss the ball with two hands against the wall, let it bounce one time after hitting the wall, and catch it with two hands. Say one letter each time the ball bounces.
3. Toss the ball to the wall and try to catch it without letting it bounce. After each toss, say one letter continuing in alphabetical order.

Skill Check

Make sure the student performs each activity with both hands.

Skills Developed

Locomotor skills, motor planning, spatial awareness

Equipment

Floor tape

Setup

Use tape to mark four lines, approximately 3 feet (1 meter) long and 3 feet apart, on the floor for each station.

Activity

1. Jump over the line on the floor with both feet.
2. With your hands on your hips, jump over the line slowly five times, then quickly five times.
3. Jump across the line high, then turn around and jump across the line high again. Repeat, jumping low this time.
4. Repeat steps 1, 2, and 3 and recite the alphabet while jumping. Say one letter after each jump.

Skill Check

Remind the student to slow down and focus on using the correct form for a standing long jump:

- Bend both knees with your arms extended behind your body before takeoff.
- When jumping, thrust your arms forcefully forward and upward (above your head).
- Take off and land with both feet.
- Move your arms downward on landing.

Skills Developed
Locomotor skills, motor planning, spatial awareness

Equipment
- Six cones with clear sleeves
- Active learning cards (uppercase letters with pictures)

Setup
Place six cones 4 feet (1.2 meters) apart in a straight line. Place matching letter and picture cards in cones, alternating with each cone: letter A, apple picture, letter B, ball picture, letter C, cat picture.

Activity
Frog-jump from cone to cone. At each cone, touch the cone and say the letter or picture shown on the card.

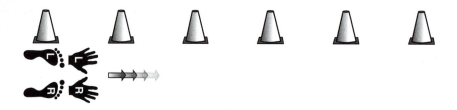

Skill Check
- Make sure that the student jumps from cone to cone rather than running.
- Remind the student to slow down and focus on using the correct form for a frog jump:
  - Start in a squat position.
  - Place your hands on the floor between your legs.
  - Move your hands to a position on the floor a short distance in front of your body.
  - Keeping your feet together and your hands on the floor, jump and let your feet land near your hands.

Skills Developed

Laterality, locomotor skills, motor planning

Equipment

- Hopscotch mat
- Active learning cards (uppercase letters with pictures)

Activity

Jump with both feet from square to square. On landing, say the letter and picture shown on the card for the square you are jumping into. (This activity is the same as the one for station 2 in week 1 except that it uses different active learning cards.)

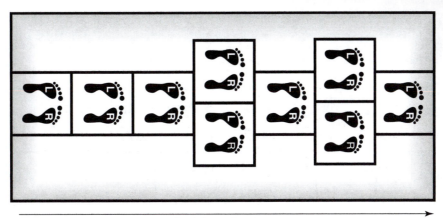

Jump in each square

Skill Check

- The student may try to do a traditional hopscotch pattern. Make sure that he or she jumps with both feet simultaneously into each square.
- Remind the student to slow down and focus on using the correct form for a standing long jump:
  - Bend both knees with your arms extended behind your body before takeoff.
  - When jumping, thrust your arms forcefully forward and upward (above your head).
  - Take off and land with both feet.
  - Move your arms downward on landing.

Skills Developed

Laterality, motor planning, gross motor coordination

Equipment

- Floor mat
- Wall mat
- Active learning cards (uppercase letters with pictures)
- Foam ball with diameter of 6 to 8 inches (15 to 20 centimeters)
- Stick-on hooks

Setup

Use stick-on hooks to hang the wall mat.

Activity

- Floor mat: Jump and land on the line at the top of each square. On each landing, say the letter and picture shown on the corresponding card.

- Wall mat: Hold the ball behind your head (as if preparing to make a soccer throw-in), then touch it to the mat two times on each uppercase letter. Each time you touch the ball to an uppercase letter, say the letter and its color.

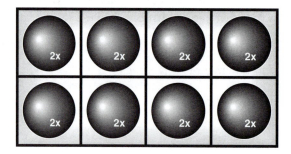

Skill Check

Remind the student to slow down and focus on using the correct form for a standing long jump:

- Bend both knees with your arms extended behind your body before takeoff.
- When jumping, thrust your arms forcefully forward and upward (above your head).
- Take off and land with both feet.
- Move your arms downward on landing.

Skills Developed

Laterality, eye–hand coordination, dynamic balance

Equipment

- Floor beam—best if about 6 feet (2 meters) long and no more than 6 inches (15 centimeters) off the floor
- Two hoops, one on either side at the middle of the floor beam
- Two beanbags
- Active learning cards (upper- and lowercase letters)

Setup

Place one hoop on either side of the floor beam as shown in the diagram. Place active learning cards in the hoops; each card shows the letter of the day (uppercase on the right side of the beam, lowercase on the left side). The cards should be changed daily to the next letter in the alphabet.

Activity

Walk forward on the beam while holding one beanbag in each hand. As you reach each pair of hoops, simultaneously drop one beanbag with each hand into each hoop (on either side of the beam). When you drop the beanbags, say the letter shown on the cards in the hoops.

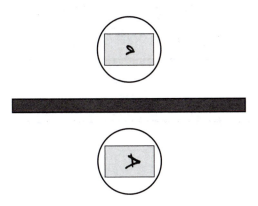

Skill Check

- Make sure that the student uses dynamic balance to maintain equilibrium while in motion. He or she may need assistance due to the challenge of holding the beanbags.
- The student should do the task smoothly, without falling or having to hold on to an object (e.g., chair or wall).
- Emphasize the correct form for walking:
  - Stand tall by keeping your body erect.
  - You should be able to draw a straight line from ear to shoulder.
  - Align your hips, knees, and ankles.
  - Your head should be level and looking forward, and your chin should be parallel to the ground.
  - Your shoulders should be relaxed and your arms bent.
  - Swing your arms in opposition to your foot movement.
  - Walk heel to toe.

Skills Developed

Body awareness, motor planning, gross motor coordination

Equipment

- Ladder mat
- Three poly spots
- Active learning cards (uppercase letters with pictures)

Setup

Place a poly spot in every other square of the ladder mat and an active learning card in each of the remaining squares.

Activity

Jump from squares without poly spots to squares without poly spots. On landing, say what is shown on each card.

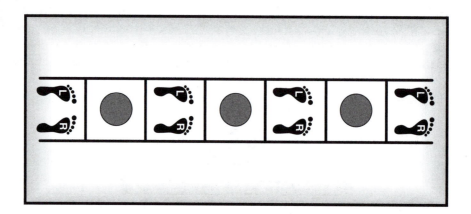

Skill Check

Remind the student to slow down and focus on using the correct form for a standing long jump:

- Bend both knees with your arms extended behind your body before takeoff.
- When jumping, thrust your arms forcefully forward and upward (above your head).
- Take off and land with both feet.
- Move your arms downward on landing.

Skills Developed

Eye–hand coordination, balance

Equipment

- One stomp board for each child
- One beanbag for each child

Activity

1. Jump softly with both feet on the stomp board to project the beanbag into the air. Cup your hands to catch the beanbag while saying a letter of the alphabet. Say a new letter with each catch attempt, going in alphabetical order. Repeat until you have tried to catch the beanbag 5 times.

2. Now, jump harder with both feet on the stomp board to project the beanbag higher into the air with each stomp. Cup your hands to catch the beanbag while saying a letter of the alphabet. Say a new letter with each catch attempt, going in alphabetical order. Repeat until you have tried to catch the beanbag 5 times.

3. Repeat these two activities until it is time to rotate stations.

Skill Check

- Make sure that the student uses both feet while stomping.
- Remind the student to slow down and focus on using the correct form for a bird's nest catch (two-hand catch with palms up).
  - Prepare by extending your hands in front of your body with your elbows bent.
  - Reach for the beanbag with your palms up as the beanbag approaches.
  - Catch the beanbag with your hands only—not against your chest.
  - Keep your eyes on the beanbag while catching it.

Skills Developed

Eye–hand coordination, spatial awareness, coordination

Equipment

- Two cones for each child
- One cone sleeve for each cone
- Active learning cards (uppercase letters with pictures)
- Floor tape
- 8.5-inch (22-centimeter) playground ball

Setup

Place two cones 3 feet (1 meter) apart from each other and 1 foot (0.3 meters) from a wall. Mark a line with floor tape 10 feet (3 meters) away from the cones. Each student has his or her own set of cones so that all four may participate at the same time.

Activity

1. Stand at the line, facing the cones and the wall. Say the uppercase letter and picture shown on each card in the cone sleeves. Place the ball on the floor between your legs and roll it (with two hands together) between the cones and toward the wall. Retrieve the ball after it rebounds from the wall. Repeat until you have rolled the ball five times.

2. Face away from the cones or wall. Say what is shown on the active learning cards. Roll the ball backward between your legs so that it goes between the cones. Retrieve the ball after it rebounds from the wall.

Skill Check

Make sure the student performs each activity with both hands.

Skills Developed

Directionality, locomotor skills

Equipment

- Jump box—a sturdy 18-inch-by-18-inch (45-centimeter) platform that is 12 inches (30 centimeters) tall and designed for students to step on and jump from
- Floor tape
- Three cones
- Incline mat
- Active learning cards (uppercase letters with pictures)

Setup

As shown in the diagram, use tape to mark three lines on the floor near the jump box: one line that is 1 foot (about 30 centimeters) from the jump box, a second line 1 foot beyond the first line, and a third line 1 foot beyond the second line. Beside each line, place a cone with an active learning card.

Activity

The activity may be done without the incline mat if one is not available. We do use the mat and children crawl up the mat to get to the jump box.

1. Get on the jump box and take the proper jumping position with both knees bent and your arms extended behind your body.
2. Jump onto the first (closest) line and say what is shown on the card with the cone for that line.
3. Jump from the first line onto the second line and say what is shown on its card.
4. Jump from the second line onto the third line and say what is shown on its card.

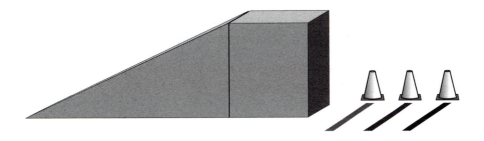

Skill Check

Remind the student to slow down and focus on using the correct form for a standing long jump:

- Bend both knees with your arms extended behind your body before takeoff.
- When jumping, thrust your arms forcefully forward and upward (above your head).
- Take off and land with both feet.
- Move your arms downward on landing.

Skills Developed

Locomotor skills, motor planning, spatial awareness

Equipment

- Six cones with clear sleeves
- Active learning cards (lowercase letters with pictures)

Setup

Place six cones 3 feet (1 meter) apart in a straight line. Place matching letter and picture cards in cones, alternating with each cone: letter A, apple picture, letter B, ball picture, letter C, cat picture.

Activity

Jump backward from cone to cone. At each cone, touch the cone and say the letter or picture shown on the card.

Jump backward

Skill Check

- Make sure that the student jumps from cone to cone rather than running.
- Remind students to watch where they are going when jumping backward.
- Remind the student to slow down and focus on using the correct form for a standing long jump:
  - Bend both knees with your arms extended behind your body before takeoff.
  - When jumping, thrust your arms forcefully forward and upward (above your head).
  - Take off and land with both feet.
  - Move your arms downward on landing.

Skills Developed

Laterality, locomotor skills, motor planning

Equipment

- Hopscotch mat
- Active learning cards (lowercase letters and spelling words)

Activity

Bunny-hop through the mat by moving hands forward one square followed by feet. Say the letter and word on the card in each square.

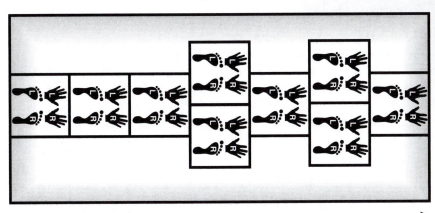

Skill Check

Make sure that the student uses correct form for a bunny hop:

- Get into a crouch position with your hands side by side and your feet side by side.
- Move both hands forward at the same time.
- Now, jump both feet forward at the same time.
- Maintain your balance and execute several consecutive bunny hops.

Skills Developed

Laterality, motor planning, gross motor coordination

Equipment

- Floor mat
- Wall mat
- Active learning cards (lowercase letters and spelling words)
- Stick-on hooks

Setup

Use stick-on hooks to hang the wall mat.

Activity

- Floor mat: Start by facing forward with both feet in the first square of the middle row. Jump forward into the next square, making a quarter-turn in the air before landing. On landing, say what is shown on the card for the square you are jumping into. Continue in this way through the rest of the squares.

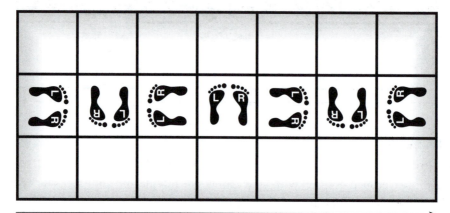

- Wall mat: Make two fists and use a punching motion to touch the mat with both hands at the same time. While touching the cards, say what each shows.

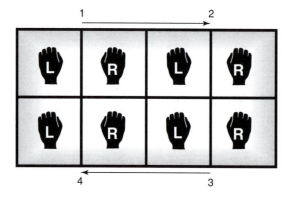

Skill Check

- Encourage the student to speak loudly when saying what is shown on the card.
- Make sure both of the student's hands touch at the same time.

Skills Developed

Laterality, locomotor skills, motor planning

Equipment

Five hoops

Setup

Place five hoops in a straight line 6 inches (15 centimeters) apart.

Activity

1. Jump forward from hoop to hoop while saying one letter in alphabetical order after each jump.
2. Jump backward from hoop to hoop while saying one letter in alphabetical order after each jump.

Skill Check

Remind students to slow down and focus on using the correct form for a standing long jump:

- Bend both knees with your arms extended behind your body before takeoff.
- When jumping, thrust your arms forcefully forward and upward (above your head).
- Take off and land with both feet.
- Move your arms downward on landing.

Skills Developed

Body awareness, motor planning, gross motor coordination

Equipment

- Ladder mat
- Active learning cards (lowercase letters and spelling words)

Activity

While saying what is shown on the cards, jump sideways from square to square along one edge of the ladder. On landing, say what is shown on the card for the square you are jumping into.

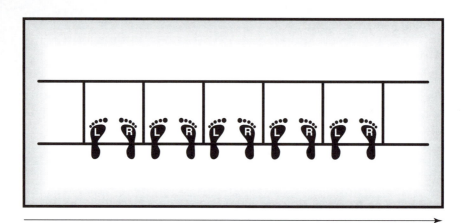

Skill Check

- The student may try to move one foot at a time. Encourage him or her to jump—not step—sideways.
- Encourage the student to slow down and say what is shown on the cards.
- Make sure that the student uses proper form for sideways jumping:
  - Make sure feet are parallel to each other with toes pointing forward,
  - When jumping, thrust your arms forcefully forward and upward (above your head).
  - Take off and land with both feet.
  - Move your arms downward on landing.

Skills Developed

Laterality, dynamic balance

Equipment

- Floor beam—best if about 6 feet (2 meters) long and no more than 6 inches (15 centimeters) off the floor
- Long noodle (approximately 3 feet (1 meter)

Activity

1. Hold a noodle horizontal in both hands with palms up at chest level and walk forward for the length of the beam.
2. Carry a noodle over your head with both hands and walk forward for the length of the beam.

Skill Check

- Make sure that the student uses dynamic balance to maintain equilibrium while in motion. He or she may need some assistance due to the challenge of holding the noodle.
- Make sure that the student uses proper form for walking:
  - Stand tall by keeping your body erect.
  - You should be able to draw a straight line from ear to shoulder.
  - Align your hips, knees, and ankles.
  - Your head should be level and looking forward, and your chin should be parallel to the ground.
  - Your shoulders should be relaxed and your arms bent.
  - Walk heel to toe.
- The student should do the task smoothly, without falling or having to hold on to an object (e.g., chair, wall).
- If a student experiences severe difficulty on the beam, allow him or her to walk on a line on the floor.

Skills Developed

Eye–hand coordination, spatial awareness, coordination

Equipment

- Four cones
- Active learning cards (lowercase letters and spelling words)
- Floor tape
- 8.5-inch (22-centimeter) playground ball

Setup

Use the floor tape to mark a line 6 feet (2 meters) away from each cone.

Activity

1. While standing, place the ball on the floor between your legs and roll it (with both hands together) at a cone. Say the letter on the cone. Retrieve the ball and repeat until you have rolled the ball five times.

2. Turn and face away from the cone. Roll the ball backward between your legs at the cone. Say the letter on the cone. Retrieve the ball and repeat until you have rolled the ball five times.

Skill Check

Make sure the student performs each activity with both hands.

Skills Developed

Directionality, locomotor skills

Equipment

- Jump box
- Incline mat
- Hoop

Activity

The activity may be done without the incline mat if one is not available. We do use the mat and children crawl up the mat to get to the jump box.

1. Get on the jump box and assume proper jumping position, with knees bent and your arms extended behind your body. Jump into the hoop, making a quarter-turn to the right in the air.

2. Get on the jump box and assume proper jumping position, with knees bent and your arms extended behind your body. Jump into the hoop, making a quarter-turn to the left.

3. Get on the jump box and assume proper jumping position, with knees bent and your arms extended behind your body. Jump into the hoop, making a half-turn in either direction in the air (so you face the jump box upon landing).

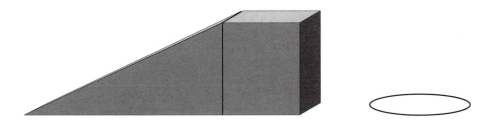

Skill Check

- Make sure that the student lands on two feet and thrusts his or her arms downward on landing.
- Remind the student to slow down and focus on using the correct form for a standing long jump:
  - Bend both knees with your arms extended behind your body before takeoff.
  - When jumping, thrust your arms forcefully forward and upward (above your head).
  - Take off and land with both feet.
  - Move your arms downward on landing.

Skills Developed

Locomotor skills, motor planning, spatial awareness

Equipment

- Six cones with clear sleeves
- Active learning cards (spelling words)

Setup

Place six cones 4 feet (1.2 meters) apart in a straight line. Place matching letter and picture cards in cones, alternating with each cone: letter A, apple picture, letter B, ball picture, letter C, cat picture.

Activity

Do bunny hops from cone to cone. At each cone, touch the cone and say the letter or picture.

Skill Check

- Make sure that the student jumps from cone to cone rather than running.
- Make sure that the student uses proper form for the bunny hop:
    - Get into a crouch position with your hands side by side on the floor.
    - Move both hands forward at the same time.
    - Now, jump both feet forward at the same time.
    - Maintain your balance and execute several consecutive bunny hops.
    - Think: "Hands first—let the feet catch up."

Skills Developed

Laterality, locomotor skills, motor planning

Equipment

- Hopscotch mat
- One beanbag for each child
- Active learning cards (uppercase letters and spelling words)

Activity

Jump 2 times in each square. On landing, say what is on the card for the square you're jumping into. Then toss and catch the beanbag 2 times.

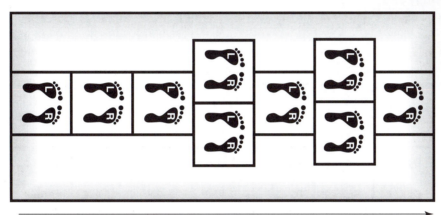

Jump 2 times in each square and toss and catch a beanbag 2 times

Skill Check

- The student may try to do a traditional hopscotch pattern. Make sure that he or she jumps with both feet simultaneously into each square.
- Remind the student to focus on using the correct form for a standing long jump:
    - Bend both knees with your arms extended behind your body before takeoff.
    - When jumping, thrust your arms forcefully forward and upward.
    - Take off and land with both feet.
    - Move your arms downward on landing.
- Remind the student to focus on using the correct form for a bird's nest catch (two-hand catch with palms up):
    - Prepare by extending your hands in front of your body with your elbows bent.
    - Reach for the beanbag with your palms up as the beanbag approaches.
    - Catch the beanbag with your hands only—not against your chest.
    - Keep your eyes on the beanbag while catching it.
- Make sure that the student uses proper form for tossing:
    - Make your tosses equally high.
    - Alternate tossing with your right and left hands.
    - Keep your eyes focused at the peak of the toss.
    - Keep your elbows close to your body.
    - Stand straight without leaning.

Skills Developed

Laterality, motor planning, gross motor coordination

Equipment

- Floor mat
- Wall mat
- Active learning cards (uppercase letters and spelling words)
- Stick-on hooks

Setup

Use stick-on hooks to hang the wall mat.

Activity

- Floor mat: Start by facing forward with both feet in the first square of the middle row. Jump forward into the next square, making a half-turn in the air before landing. On landing, say the letter and word shown on the card for the square you're jumping into. Continue in this way through the rest of the squares.

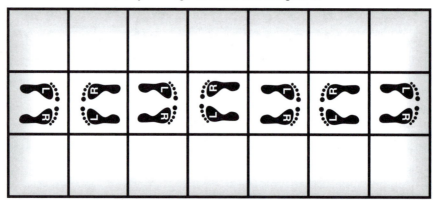

- Wall mat: Point your right and left index fingers and touch both to the upper left square of the mat. Say the letter and word shown on the corresponding card. Continue across the top row of the mat, moving left to right, and then the bottom row of the mat, moving right to left.

Skill Check

- Encourage the student to speak loudly when saying what is shown on the card.
- Ensure that the student touches both hands to the wall mat at the same time.
- Remind the student to slow down and focus on using the correct form for a standing long jump:
  - Bend both knees with your arms extended behind your body before takeoff.
  - When jumping, thrust your arms forcefully forward and upward (above your head).
  - Take off and land with both feet.
  - Move your arms downward on landing.

Skills Developed

Laterality, locomotor skills, motor planning

Equipment

- Hoops
- Floor pattern cards (available on the web resource)

Setup

Choose a floor pattern card and arrange hoops as shown on that card.

Activity

1. Jump from one hoop to the next with two feet.
2. Repeat the activity with different cards as long as time permits.

Skill Check

- Make sure the student reproduces the pattern correctly.
- Remind the student to slow down and focus on using the correct form for a standing long jump:
  - Bend both knees with your arms extended behind your body before takeoff.
  - When jumping, thrust your arms forcefully forward and upward (above your head).
  - Take off and land with both feet.
  - Move your arms downward on landing.

Skills Developed

Body awareness, motor planning, gross motor coordination

Equipment

- Ladder mat
- Active learning cards (uppercase letters and spelling words)

Activity

Jump sideways with both feet, making a quarter-turn to the right in the air. Then jump sideways with both feet, making a quarter-turn back to the left in the air. Continue this pattern to the end of the mat.

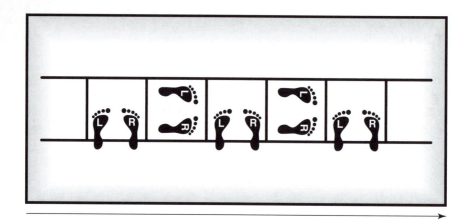

Skill Check

Remind the student to slow down and focus on using the correct form for a standing long jump:

- Bend both knees with your arms extended behind your body before takeoff.
- When jumping, thrust your arms forcefully forward and upward (above your head).
- Take off and land with both feet.
- Move your arms downward on landing.

Skills Developed

Spatial awareness, directionality, arm strength, leg strength

Equipment

- One scooter board for each student
- Five cones with clear sleeves
- Active learning cards (uppercase letters and spelling words)

Setup

Place five cones in a straight line 3 feet (1 meter) apart.

Activity

1. Lie on your tummy on the scooter board and push with both hands to weave through the sequence of cones. As you pass each cone, say what is shown on the card for that cone.

2. Sit on the scooter board and push with both feet to weave backward through the sequence of cones. As you pass each cone, say what is shown on the card for that cone.

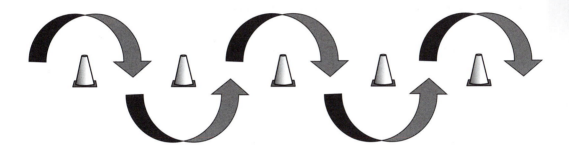

Skill Check

- Stress scooter board safety (e.g., never stand on the board, keep hands on the side, keep hair and clothing away from the wheels).
- Make sure the student stays on his or her tummy and uses both hands to push in the first part of the activity and both feet to push in the second part.

Skills Developed

Kinesthetic awareness, tactile awareness, locomotor skills

Equipment

- Jump box—a sturdy 18-inch-by-18-inch (45-centimeter) platform that is 12 inches (30 centimeters) tall and designed for students to step on and jump from
- Four cones
- Active learning cards (uppercase letters and spelling words)
- Incline ramp (optional)
- Floor tape

Setup

As shown in the diagram, use tape to mark four lines in a row on the floor at the following distances from the jump box: 12 inches (about 30 centimeters), 14 inches (36 centimeters), 16 inches (41 centimeters), and 18 inches (46 centimeters). Beside each line, place a cone with an active learning card.

Activity

The activity may be done without the incline mat if one is not available. We do use the mat and children crawl up the mat to get to the jump box.

1. Get on the jump box and take the proper jumping position, with both knees bent and your arms extended behind your body.
2. Jump onto the closest line and say what is shown on the card for the cone next to that line.
3. Get on the jump box and take the proper jumping position, with both knees bent and your arms extended behind your body. Jump on the second line and say what is shown on the card for the cone next to that line.
4. Get on the jump box and take the proper jumping position, with both knees bent and your arms extended behind your body. Jump onto the third line and say what is shown on the card for the cone next to that line.
5. Get on the jump box and take the proper jumping position, with both knees bent and your arms extended behind your body. Jump onto the fourth line and say what is shown on the card for the cone next to that line.

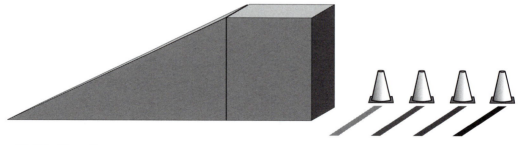

Skill Check

Remind the student to focus on using the correct form for a standing long jump:

- Bend both knees with your arms extended behind your body before takeoff.
- When jumping, thrust your arms forcefully forward and upward (above your head).
- Take off and land with both feet.
- Move your arms downward on landing.

Skills Developed

Eye–hand coordination, spatial awareness, directionality

Equipment

- Four hoops, 28 to 30 inches (71 to 76 centimeters) in diameter
- One 8.5-inch (22-centimeter) playground ball for each child

Setup

Position hoops in a scattered formation leaving 4 feet (1.2 meters) between hoops.

Activity

1. Walk to each hoop and use both hands to bounce and catch the ball inside of the hoop. Each time you bounce the ball, say a letter in alphabetical order.
2. Sit outside the hoop and use both your feet at the same time to roll the ball around the inside of the hoop.

Skill Check

- The student should bounce the ball with finger pads (no slapping) and keep the ball under control.
- Make sure that the student uses both feet simultaneously.

3

UNILATERAL ACTIVITIES

Movement requires and encourages the transfer of information between the two brain hemispheres. In other words, young children must move in order to learn; sitting still puts a strain on a child. Unilateral activities aid in hemispheric brain development by isolating one side of the body to develop each side of the brain. This gets children ready to learn or gets their brain ready to cross hemispheres. Specific isolation of one side of the body helps develop neural pathways in the brain by activating the vestibular with activities that require balance. These activities include hopping, unilateral crawl and walk, and tossing objects into targets (stepping and tossing with the same foot and hand). Both hemispheres of the brain are being used by isolating each side during each activity. In the activities listed in this chapter the students will use one side of the body, and on the next turn will do the activity with the other side of the body, alternating sides until the music stops.

Use the following guide to choosing the appropriate active learning cards for each week:

Week 1: Colors and shapes

Week 2: Numbers

Week 3: Lowercase letters

Week 4: Lowercase letters with pictures

Week 5: Uppercase letters

Week 6: Uppercase letters with pictures

Week 7: Lowercase letters and spelling words

Week 8: Uppercase letters and spelling words

Although these categories give you general guidelines to go by, some specific activities might call for a different category than described here.

UNILATERAL ACTIVITIES

Skills Developed

Laterality, motor planning, gross motor coordination

Equipment

- One tumbling mat
- Four cones
- Active learning cards (colors and shapes)

Setup

Place cones in a straight line 2 feet (0.6 meter) apart on the mat. (Photo shows a variant setup in which cones are staggered.)

Activity

1. Do a unilateral crawl from cone to cone by using your right hand and right leg at the same time and then your left hand and left leg at the same time. As you pass each cone, say what is shown on the card for that cone.
2. Once you reach the last cone, do a backward unilateral crawl to your original starting point by using your left hand and left leg at the same time and then your right hand and right leg at the same time.

Skill Check

- The student should raise his or her torso so that the weight is supported by the hands and knees without the stomach touching the floor.
- Movement should be continual.
- The relevant hand and knee should move forward simultaneously.

Skills Developed

Laterality, locomotor skills, spatial awareness, motor planning

Equipment

- Hopscotch mat
- Active learning cards (colors and shapes)

Activity

Hop through the mat using only your left foot. With each hop, say what is shown on the card for the square you are landing in. Repeat the activity using only your right foot. Continue in this way—hopping through the mat on your left foot, then hopping through on your right foot, then back to the left, and so on.

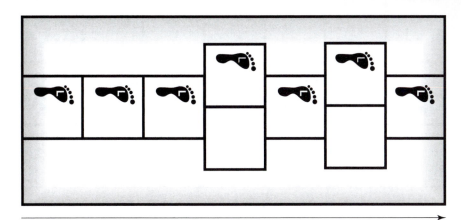

Skill Check

- The student should hop on only one foot in each square, thus isolating that side of the body.
- Make sure that the student uses proper hopping form:
  - Swing your non-weight-bearing leg like a pendulum to produce power.
  - On landing, keep the foot of your non-weight-bearing leg behind your body.
  - Bend your arms and swing them forward to produce power.

Skills Developed

Laterality, locomotor skills, motor planning

Equipment

- Floor mat
- Wall mat
- Active learning cards (colors and shapes)

Activity

- Floor mat: Gallop through the squares, always keeping the same foot in front. As you land in each square, say what is shown on the card for that square.

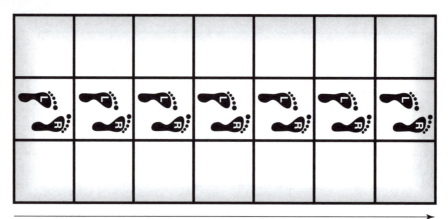

Gallop through the squares

- Wall mat: Starting at the top left corner of the mat, touch every square in the top row with your right hand. Then come back across the mat, this time on the bottom row, using your left hand. Each time you touch a square, say what is shown on the card for that square.

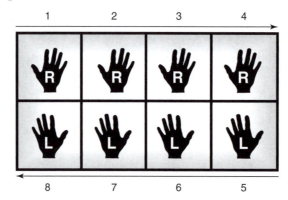

Skill Check

- Encourage the student to speak loudly in saying what is shown on the card.
- Make sure that the student uses proper form for galloping:
    - To begin, flex your arms and hold them at waist level.
    - Take a starting stance with your right foot in front of your left. Step forward with your front foot, then bring your back foot next to or just behind your lead foot.
    - Next comes a brief period when both of your feet are off the floor.
    - Move your feet with a rhythmic pattern.

Skills Developed

Spatial awareness, eye–hand coordination, body awareness, gross motor coordination

Equipment

- One hoop for each student
- One 8.5-inch (22-centimeter) playground ball for each student

Activity

1. Crawl around the outside of the hoop while rolling the ball around inside the hoop with the fingertips of one hand.
2. Crawl around the outside of the hoop while rolling the ball around inside the hoop with an elbow.
3. Reverse the direction of the crawl, using the other side. Roll the ball with the hand closest to the ball.

Skill Check

Make sure the student uses proper crawling form:

- Raise your torso so that your weight is supported by your hands and knees without your stomach touching the floor.
- Movement should be continual.
- Your right hand and right knee (and your left hand and left knee) should move forward simultaneously.

Skills Developed

Laterality, motor planning, dynamic balance

Equipment

Ladder mat

Activity

Hop on the rungs of the ladder on your right foot. On each landing, say the color of that rung. Repeat using the left foot to hop.

Skill Check

Make sure that the student uses proper hopping form:

- Swing your non-weight-bearing leg like a pendulum to produce power.
- On landing, keep the foot of your non-weight-bearing leg behind your body.
- Bend your arms and swing them forward to produce power.

Skills Developed

Laterality, locomotor skills, motor planning

Equipment

- Agility rings (A round ring used for agility training or juggling. These rings can be found in any of the physical education catalogues stated in chapter 1.)
- Active learning cards (uppercase letters with pictures)

Setup

Place the rings on the floor so that they are touching one another. Place an active learning card in each ring.

Activity

Hop forward three rings, saying the letter shown on the card for each ring as you land in it. Then hop to the next ring and say what is shown in the picture on the card. Continue on to the next letter–picture sequence.

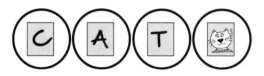

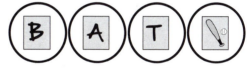

Skill Check

Make sure that the student uses proper hopping form:

- Swing your non-weight-bearing leg like a pendulum to produce power.
- On landing, keep the foot of your non-weight-bearing leg behind your body.
- Bend your arms and swing them forward to produce power.

Skills Developed

Unilateral movement, balance

Equipment

- Two buckets
- Two beanbags
- Floor tape

Setup

Tape a thick line on the floor to represent a balance beam; make the line 2 inches (5 centimeters) thick and 6 feet (2 meters) long. At one end of the line, place a bucket containing two beanbags. At the other end of the line, place an empty bucket.

Activity

Walk on the line while carrying a bucket containing two beanbags in your nondominant hand. At the end of the line, take the beanbags out of the bucket you are holding and use an underhand toss to toss them into the empty bucket while maintaining your balance. Retrieve the beanbags and walk on the line back to the beginning. Repeat the activity.

Skill Check

- Make sure that the student stays on the line while walking heel to toe.
- Make sure that the student tosses before stepping off the line.
- Make sure that the student uses proper form for walking:
    - Stand tall by keeping your body erect.
    - You should be able to draw a straight line from ear to shoulder.
    - Align your hips, knees, and ankles.
    - Your head should be level and looking forward, and your chin should be parallel to the ground.
    - Your shoulders should be relaxed and your arms bent.
    - Swing your arms in opposition to your foot movement.
    - Walk heel to toe.
- Make sure that the student uses proper form for the underhand toss:
    - Face the target.
    - Step with the foot on the opposite side from your throwing hand.
    - Bring your arm back, then swing it forward and release the ball.

Skills Developed

Laterality, dynamic balance, directionality

Equipment

Floor beam

Activity

1. Stand sideways on the beam and slide to the right. Slide your right foot out until your feet are shoulder width apart, then slide your left foot to catch up. Each time you move, say "right."

2. Stand sideways on the beam and slide back to the left to where you started. Slide your left foot out until your feet are shoulder width apart, then slide your right foot to catch up. Each time you move, say "left."

Skill Check

- Make sure that the student uses proper sliding form:
  - Turn your body sideways (shoulders aligned with the beam, toes pointed perpendicular to the beam).
  - Step sideways with your leading foot, then slide your trailing foot to meet it.
  - Move with a rhythmic continual motion.
- Make sure that the student uses dynamic balance (balance while in motion) to maintain equilibrium while in motion. He or she may need assistance due to the challenge of holding the beanbags.
- The student should do the task smoothly, without falling or having to hold on to an object (e.g., chair or wall).

Skills Developed

Laterality, motor planning, gross motor coordination

Equipment

- Six cones
- Six cone collars
- Active learning cards (numbers)

Setup

Place the cones 4 feet (1.2 meters) apart and in a line.

Activity

1. Walk unilaterally from cone to cone by moving your right arm and your right leg at the same time. As you reach each cone, say what is shown on its card.
2. Walk backward unilaterally.

Skill Check

Make sure that the student uses proper unilateral walking form:

- Stand tall by keeping your body erect (imagine a straight line drawn from either ear to the shoulder on the same side).
- Align your hips, knees, and ankles.
- Keep your head level and look forward with your chin parallel to the ground.
- Let your shoulders relax and bend your arms.
- Move the arm and foot on the same side of your body at the same time.
- Walk heel to toe.

Skills Developed

Laterality, locomotor skills, spatial awareness, motor planning

Equipment

- Hopscotch mat
- Active learning cards (numbers)

Activity

Hop through the mat using only your left foot. With each hop, say what is shown on the card for the square you are landing in. Repeat the activity using only your right foot. Continue in this way—hopping through the mat on your left foot, then hopping through on your right foot, then on the left, and so on. (This activity is the same as the one for week 1, station 2.)

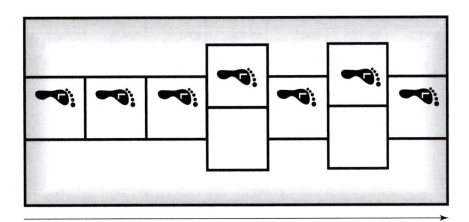

Skill Check

- The student should hop on only one foot in each square, thus isolating that side of the body.
- Make sure that the student uses proper hopping form:
    - Swing your non-weight-bearing leg like a pendulum to produce power.
    - On landing, keep the foot of your non-weight-bearing leg behind your body.
    - Bend your arms and swing them forward to produce power.

Skills Developed

Laterality, locomotor skills, motor planning

Equipment

- Floor mat
- Wall mat
- Active learning cards (numbers)

Activity

- Floor mat: Gallop through the squares, always keeping the same foot in front; as you gallop, tap both hands on your forward leg. As you land in each square, say what is shown on the card for that square.

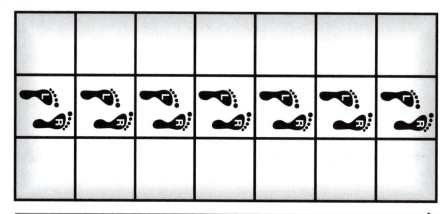

Tap both hands on the forward leg while galloping

- Wall mat: Starting at the top left square, use your left hand to touch the top square and then the bottom square in each column of the mat (working from left to right). Each time you touch a square, say what is shown on the card for that square. When you reach the end of the mat, switch hands and work back across the mat (right to left) in the same top-to-bottom pattern.

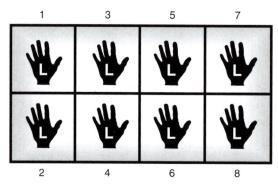

Skill Check

Make sure that the student uses proper form for galloping:

- To begin, flex your arms and hold them at waist level.
- Start with your feet together. Step forward with one foot (this will be your lead foot), then bring your other foot next to or just behind your lead foot.
- Next comes a brief period when both of your feet are off the floor.
- Move your feet with a rhythmic pattern.

Skills Developed

Spatial awareness, gross motor coordination

Equipment

- Hoop
- 8.5-inch (22-centimeter) playground ball
- Long noodle

Activity

1. Crawl around the outside of the hoop while rolling the ball around inside of the hoop with one hand.
2. Walk around the outside of the hoop while using the noodle to roll the ball around inside of the hoop.
3. After you go around the hoop one full time, reverse direction and repeat steps 1 and 2.

Skill Check

- Make sure that the student uses only one hand to roll and one hand to hold the noodle.
- Make sure that the student uses proper form for walking:
  - Stand tall by keeping your body erect.
  - You should be able to draw a straight line from ear to shoulder.
  - Align your hips, knees, and ankles.
  - Your head should be level and looking forward, and your chin should be parallel to the ground.
  - Your shoulders should be relaxed and your arms bent.
  - Swing your arms in opposition to your foot movement.
  - Walk heel to toe.

Skills Developed

Laterality, motor planning, gross motor coordination, dynamic balance

Equipment

Ladder mat

Activity

Hop on the rungs of the ladder on your left foot. On each landing, say the color of that rung. Repeat this activity using your other foot. (This activity is the same as the one for station 5 in week 1.)

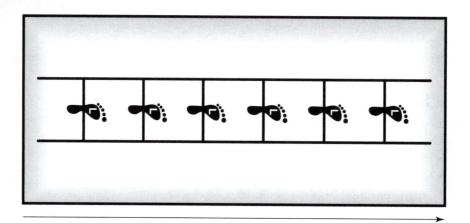

Skill Check

Make sure that the student uses proper hopping form:

- Swing your non-weight-bearing leg like a pendulum to produce power.
- On landing, keep the foot of your non-weight-bearing leg behind your body.
- Bend your arms and swing them forward to produce power.

Skills Developed

Laterality, locomotor skills, motor planning

Equipment

- Agility rings
- Floor pattern cards (available on the web resource)

Activity

1. Choose a floor pattern card and arrange the rings on the floor in the pattern shown on the card. Hop forward through the rings, using one foot and then the other.

2. Step sideways through the rings with your hands on your knees.

Skill Check

Make sure that the student uses proper hopping form:

- Swing your non-weight-bearing leg like a pendulum to produce power.
- On landing, keep the foot of your non-weight-bearing leg behind your body.
- Bend your arms and swing them forward to produce power.

Skills Developed

Laterality, dynamic balance, directionality

Equipment

- Floor beam
- Beanbag

Activity

1. While holding a beanbag in your right hand, stand sideways on the beam and slide to the right. Slide your right foot out until your feet are shoulder width apart, then slide your left foot to catch up. Each time you move, say "right."

2. While holding a beanbag in your left hand, stand sideways on the beam and slide to the left. Slide your left foot out until your feet are shoulder width apart, then slide your right foot to catch up. Each time you move, say "left."

Skill Check

- Make sure that the student says the relevant direction (left or right) and holds the beanbag in the corresponding hand.
- Make sure that the student uses proper sliding form:
  - Turn your body sideways (shoulders aligned with the beam, toes pointed perpendicular to the beam).
  - Step sideways with your leading foot, then slide your trailing foot to meet it.
  - Move with a rhythmic continual motion.
- Make sure that the student uses dynamic balance to maintain equilibrium while in motion. He or she may need assistance due to the challenge of holding the beanbags.
- The student should do the task smoothly, without falling or having to hold on to an object (e.g., chair or wall).

Skills Developed

Laterality, precision

Equipment

- One 8.5-inch (22-centimeter) playground ball for each student
- One plastic bowling pin or foam brick for each student
- Floor tape

Setup

Tape a line on the floor with floor tape so the student has a visual of where to roll the ball to the target. The student should be positioned about 10 feet away from their pin.

Activity

While kneeling, roll your ball to your pin or brick. Retrieve your ball, set up your brick or pin if it was knocked over, and return to roll again. Roll as many times as you can while the station music is playing.

Skill Check

Make sure the student uses proper underhand rolling form from the kneeling position:

- Face your target.
- Use a pendulum motion with your arm to roll the ball (as in bowling).
- Release the ball close to the ground.
- Follow through with your rolling hand toward the sky or ceiling.

Skills Developed

Laterality, motor planning, gross motor coordination

Equipment

- One tumbling mat
- Four cones
- Four cone collars
- Active learning cards (lowercase letters)

Setup

Place cones in a straight line 2 feet (0.6 meter) apart on the mat.

Activity

1. Do a unilateral crawl from cone to cone by using your right hand and right leg at the same time and then your left hand and left leg at the same time. As you pass each cone, say what is shown on the card for that cone.

2. Once you reach the last cone, do a backward unilateral crawl to your original starting point by using your left hand and left leg at the same time and then your right hand and right leg at the same time.

Skill Check

- The student should raise his or her torso so that the weight is supported by the hands and knees without the stomach touching the floor.
- Movement should be continual.
- The relevant hand and knee should move forward simultaneously.

Skills Developed

Laterality, locomotor skills, spatial awareness, motor planning

Equipment

- Hopscotch mat
- Active learning cards (at instructor's discretion)

Activity

Hop through the mat using only your left foot. With each hop, say what is shown on the card for the square you are landing in. Now turn around and hop back using only your right foot. As before, say what is shown on the card for each square you land in.

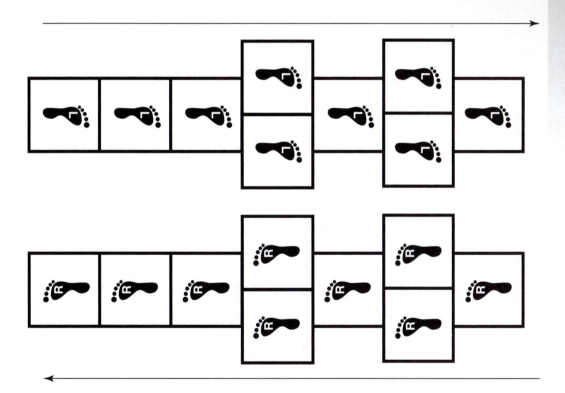

Skill Check

- The student should hop on only one foot in each square, thus isolating that side of the body.
- Make sure that the student uses proper hopping form:
  - Swing your non-weight-bearing leg like a pendulum to produce power.
  - On landing, keep the foot of your non-weight-bearing leg behind your body.
  - Bend your arms and swing them forward to produce power.

Skills Developed

Laterality, locomotor skills, motor planning

Equipment

- Floor mat
- Wall mat
- Active learning cards (lowercase letters)

Activity

- Floor mat: Hop from square to square in a zigzag pattern (diagonal left, diagonal right, diagonal left, and so on). As you land in each square, say what is shown on the card for that square. Hop with one foot all the way through, then the other foot all the way through.

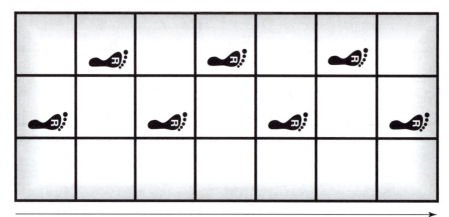

- Wall mat: Moving from left to right across the mat, use one hand to touch squares in a zigzag pattern (down to the right, up to the right, down to the right). Each time you touch a square, say what is shown on the card for that square. Switch hands and work back across the mat (down to the left, up to the left, down to the left) while saying what is shown on the card for each square as you touch it.

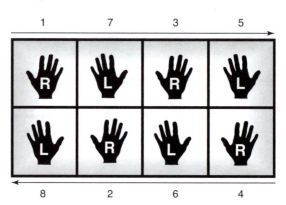

Skill Check

- The student should hop on only one foot in each square, thus isolating that side of the body.
- Make sure that the student uses proper hopping form:
  - Swing your non-weight-bearing leg like a pendulum to produce power.
  - On landing, keep the foot of your non-weight-bearing leg behind your body.
  - Bend your arms and swing them forward to produce power.

Skills Developed

Laterality, motor planning, coordination

Equipment

One Foo-Foo wand for each student

Activity

1. Lie on your back and hold the Foo-Foo wand in your right hand. Move your right arm and right leg (as in making a snow angel) while trying to touch the wand to your right heel.
2. Do the same movement with your left arm and left leg.

Skill Check

Make sure that the student moves the arm and leg on the same side of his or her body and tries to touch the wand to the heel.

Skills Developed

Laterality, locomotor skills, motor planning

Equipment

- Ladder mat
- Active learning cards (lowercase letters)

Activity

Hop from square to square between the rungs of the ladder. On each landing, say what is shown on the card for the square you land in. Hop on one foot all the way through, then on the other foot all the way through.

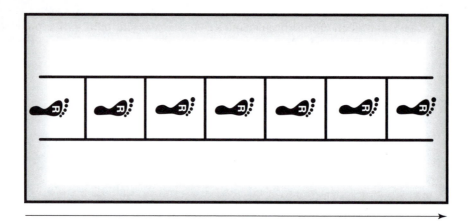

Skill Check

- The student should hop on only one foot in each square, thus isolating that side of the body.
- Make sure that the student uses proper hopping form:
  - Swing your non-weight-bearing leg like a pendulum to produce power.
  - On landing, keep the foot of your non-weight-bearing leg behind your body.
  - Bend your arms and swing them forward to produce power.

Skill Developed

Laterality, locomotor skills, motor planning

Equipment

Agility rings

Setup

Place rings in a line so that they are touching one another.

Activity

1. Hop sideways through the rings, skipping a ring with each hop.
2. Step sideways through the rings with your hands on your knees. Lead with your right foot, then catch up with your left. Once you reach the end, stay facing the same direction and step sideways to your *left* to return to your starting position (lead with your left foot, then catch up with your right).
3. Hop through the rings, saying the color of each ring as you get to it.
4. Hop through the rings, counting the rings along the way.

Skill Check

Make sure that the student uses proper hopping form:

- Swing your non-weight-bearing leg like a pendulum to produce power.
- On landing, keep the foot of your non-weight-bearing leg behind your body.
- Bend your arms and swing them forward to produce power.

Skills Developed

Laterality, eye–hand coordination, tracking skills

Equipment

- Four plastic paddles
- Four beanbags

Activity

1. Place a beanbag on the paddle and hold the paddle in your dominant hand. Use the paddle to toss and catch the beanbag. Count aloud how many tosses you can catch in a row. Repeat with your nondominant hand.

2. For a variation, say the letters of the alphabet, one letter per toss.

3. For an advanced variation, use the paddle to toss the beanbag, then hit the beanbag against the wall.

Skill Check

Remind students to flip the beanbag like a pancake.

Skills Developed

Laterality, dynamic balance, directionality

Equipment

- Floor beam
- Bucket
- Beanbags

Activity

1. While carrying a bucket in your right hand, stand sideways on the beam and slide to the right. Slide your right foot out until your feet are shoulder width apart, then slide your left foot to catch up. Each time you move, say "right." To make the bucket heavier, add beanbags. When you reach the end of the beam, get off and start over again.

2. While carrying a bucket in your left hand, stand sideways on the beam and slide to the left. Slide your left foot out until your feet are shoulder width apart, then slide your right foot to catch up. Each time you move, say "left." To make the bucket heavier, add beanbags.

Skill Check

- Make sure that the student says the relevant direction (left or right) and holds the beanbag in the corresponding hand.
- Make sure that the student uses proper sliding form:
  - Turn your body sideways (shoulders aligned with the beam, toes pointed perpendicular to the beam).
  - Step sideways with your leading foot, then slide your trailing foot to meet it.
  - Move with a rhythmic continual motion.
- Make sure that the student uses dynamic balance to maintain equilibrium while in motion. He or she may need assistance due to the challenge of holding the beanbags.
- The student should do the task smoothly, without falling or having to hold on to an object (e.g., chair or wall).

Skills Developed

Laterality, motor planning, gross motor coordination

Equipment

- Cones
- Cone collars
- Active learning cards (lowercase letters with pictures)

Activity

1. Walk unilaterally from cone to cone by moving your right arm and your right leg at the same time. As you reach each cone, say what is shown on its card.
2. Walk backward unilaterally.

Skill Check

Make sure that the student uses proper unilateral walking form:

- Stand tall by keeping your body erect (imagine a straight line drawn from either ear to the shoulder on the same side).
- Align your hips, knees, and ankles.
- Keep your head level and look forward with your chin parallel to the ground.
- Let your shoulders relax and bend your arms.
- Move the arm and foot on the same side of your body at the same time.
- Walk heel to toe.

Skills Developed

Laterality, locomotor skills, motor planning, spatial awareness

Equipment

- Hopscotch mat
- Active learning cards (lowercase letters with pictures)

Activity

Hop sideways through the mat using only your left foot. With each hop, say what is shown on the card for the square you are landing in. Repeat the activity using only your right foot.

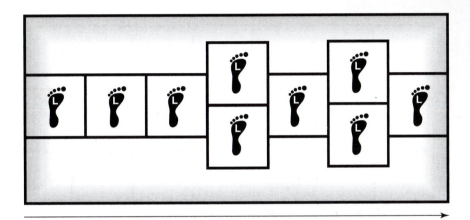

Skill Check

- The student should hop on only one foot in each square, thus isolating that side of the body.
- Make sure that the student uses proper hopping form:
  - Swing your non-weight-bearing leg like a pendulum to produce power.
  - On landing, keep the foot of your non-weight-bearing leg behind your body.
  - Bend your arms and swing them forward to produce power.

Skills Developed

Laterality, locomotor skills, motor planning

Equipment

- Floor mat
- Wall mat

Activity

- Floor mat: Move through the mat by taking large backward steps to skip over one square with each step. Place your right hand on your right knee and your left hand on your left knee.

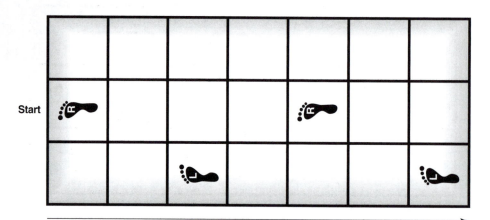

- Wall mat: Hop five times on your left foot, then touch the mat with your left hand. On your next turn, use your right foot and right hand.

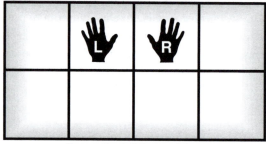

Hop on the left foot and then
touch the wall mat with the left hand;
repeat with right foot and hand

Skill Check

- Make sure that the student uses proper hopping form:
  - Swing your non-weight-bearing leg like a pendulum to produce power.
  - On landing, keep the foot of your non-weight-bearing leg behind your body.
  - Bend your arms and swing them forward to produce power.
- When touching the wall mat, make sure the student is touching the mat with the hand that matches the foot they are hopping on (e.g., left hand touches mat while the student is hopping on the left foot).

Skills Developed

Eye–hand coordination

Equipment

Cup-and-ball set

Activity

1. Swing the ball with your right hand and try to catch it in the cup. Count aloud how many times you catch the ball.

2. Repeat with your left hand.

Skill Check

Make sure that the student uses only one hand at a time and keeps count of how many times he or she catches the ball.

Skills Developed

Laterality, locomotor skills, motor planning

Equipment

- Ladder mat
- Active learning cards (at instructor's discretion)

Activity

1. Stand facing sideways on the right edge of the ladder and slide along the edge to your right. Slide your right foot out until your feet are shoulder width apart, then slide your left foot to catch up. As you slide by each square, say what is shown on the card for that square.

2. Once you reach the end, stay facing the same direction and slide back along the edge to your left in order to return to your starting position. Slide your left foot out until your feet are shoulder width apart, then slide your right foot to catch up. As you slide by each square, say what is shown on the card for that square.

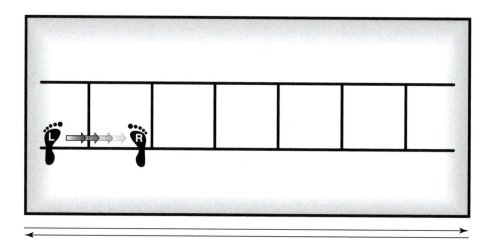

Skill Check

Make sure that the student uses proper sliding form:

- Turn your body sideways (shoulders aligned with the line, toes pointed perpendicular to the beam).
- Step sideways with your leading foot, then slide your trailing foot to meet it.
- Move with a rhythmic continual motion.

Skills Developed

Laterality, motor planning, gross motor coordination

Equipment

- One scooter board for each student
- Jump rope (10 feet or 3 meters long)
- Volleyball standard or similar apparatus

Setup

Attach the rope to the base of the volleyball standard or similar apparatus and lay it (fully extended) on the floor. Position the scooter at the free end of the rope.

Activity

1. Lie on your torso on the scooter board and use the rope to pull yourself forward with only your right hand.
2. Repeat using only your left hand.
3. Sit on the scooter board and use the rope to pull yourself forward with only your right hand.
4. Repeat using only your left hand.

Skill Check

- Stress scooter board safety (e.g., never stand on the board, keep hands on the rope, keep hair and clothing away from the wheels).
- Make sure that the student isolates one side of the body by using only one hand to pull himself or herself.

Skills Developed

Laterality, eye–foot coordination

Equipment

White and black foam bricks (five each)

Setup

Arrange two rows of bricks—the right one containing white bricks and the left one containing black bricks. In each row, the bricks should be 2 feet (0.6 meter) apart. Stagger the spacing of the two rows as shown in the illustration.

Activity

Walk between the two rows of bricks, kicking the black ones over with your left foot and kicking the white ones over with your right foot.

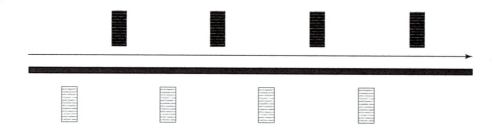

Skill Check

Make sure that the student kicks each brick with the proper foot (left foot for black bricks, right foot for white bricks).

Skills Developed

Laterality, motor planning, coordination

Equipment

- One hula hoop for each student
- Flying disc (e.g., Frisbee)
- Floor tape

Setup

Place the hoops on the floor against a wall. The hoops should be in a row about 3 feet (0.9 meter) apart from each other. Use the floor tape to mark a line approximately 5 feet (1.5 meters) away from the hoops.

Activity

1. Toss the disc into the target using your right hand and stepping with your right foot.
2. Do the same with your left hand and left foot.

Skill Check

- Make sure that the student isolates one side by stepping and throwing with the same hand and foot.
- Make sure that the student uses proper form for tossing the disc:
  - Turn your throwing hand so the palm faces up. Hold the flying disc with your index (pointer) finger on the outside rim of the disc, your other three fingers on the bottom side, and your thumb on the top side.
  - Keep your palm up and the elbow of your throwing arm in toward your body (but not tight).
  - Face the target and step toward it with the foot on the same side as your throwing hand, then toss the disc.
  - Snap your wrists and fingers on the follow-through; keep your palm up throughout the throw.

Skills Developed

Locomotor skills, motor planning

Equipment

- Six cones
- Six cone collars
- Active learning cards (uppercase letters with pictures)

Setup

Place six cones approximately 4 feet (1.2 meters) apart in a straight line. Place matching letter and picture cards in the cones, alternating with each cone—for example, letter A, apple picture, letter B, ball picture.

Activity

Hop from cone to cone. At each cone, say the letter or picture shown on the card for that cone.

Skill Check

Make sure that the student uses proper hopping form:

- Swing your non-weight-bearing leg like a pendulum to produce power.
- On landing, keep the foot of your non-weight-bearing leg behind your body.
- Bend your arms and swing them forward to produce power.

Skills Developed

Laterality, locomotor skills, motor planning, spatial awareness

Equipment

- Hopscotch mat
- Active learning cards (uppercase letters)

Activity

Hop sideways through the mat using only your left foot. With each hop, say what is shown on the card for the square you are landing in. Return to the beginning of the mat and repeat the activity using only your right foot. (This activity is the same as the one for week 4, station 2 except that it uses different active learning cards.)

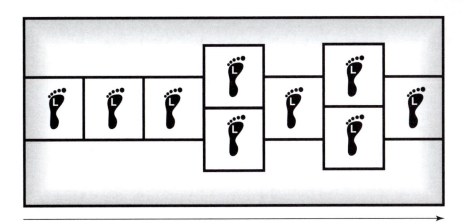

Skill Check

- The student should hop on only one foot in each square, thus isolating that side of the body.
- Make sure that the student uses proper hopping form:
  - Swing your non-weight-bearing leg like a pendulum to produce power.
  - On landing, keep the foot of your non-weight-bearing leg behind your body.
  - Bend your arms and swing them forward to produce power.

Skills Developed

Laterality, dynamic balance, motor planning

Equipment

- Floor mat
- Wall mat
- Active learning cards (uppercase letters)

Activity

- Floor mat: Hop two squares forward, then one square back. After each hop, say what is shown on the card. Repeat this pattern to the end of the mat. Now do the same sequence while hopping on your other foot.

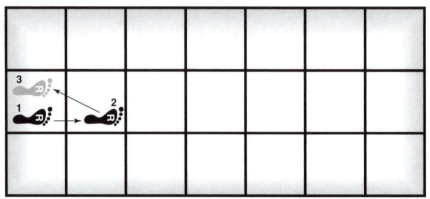

Hop forward 2 squares, then back 1 square

- Wall mat: Use one hand to touch one corner square of the mat. While touching the square, say what is shown on the card. Do the same for the other three corners. Now do all four corners with your other hand.

Skill Check

Make sure that the student uses proper hopping form:

- Swing your non-weight-bearing leg like a pendulum to produce power.
- On landing, keep the foot of your non-weight-bearing leg behind your body.
- Bend your arms and swing them forward to produce power.

Skills Developed

Transference, motor planning

Equipment

- One Foo-Foo wand for each student
- Foam geometric shapes or active learning cards (shapes)

Activity

Trace the foam shape or shape on the active learning cards with your Foo-Foo wand using large movements in the air while saying the name of the shape.

Skill Check

Make sure the student holds the wand in one hand and says aloud the name of each shape while tracing it.

Skills Developed

Laterality, locomotor skills, motor planning

Equipment

- Ladder mat
- Active learning cards (uppercase letters)

Activity

1. Stand sideways on the right edge of the ladder and slide along the edge to your right. Slide your right foot out until your feet are shoulder width apart, then slide your left foot to catch up. As you slide by each square, say what is shown on the card for that square.

2. Once you reach the end, stay facing the same direction and slide back along the edge to your left in order to return to your starting position. Slide your left foot out until your feet are shoulder width apart, then slide your right foot to catch up. As you slide by each square, say what is shown on the card for that square. (This activity is the same as for station 5 in week 4.)

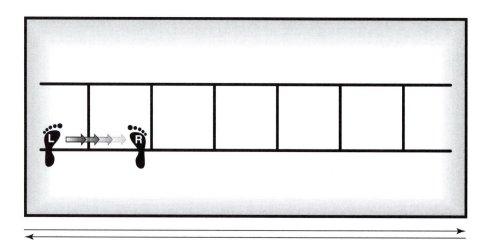

Skill Check

Make sure that the student uses proper sliding form:

- Turn your body sideways (shoulders aligned with the line, toes pointed perpendicular to the beam).
- Step sideways with your leading foot, then slide your trailing foot to meet it.
- Move with a rhythmic continual motion.

Skills Developed

Laterality, locomotor skills, motor planning

Equipment

- One ring toss set or beanbags with target (hula hoop) for each student
- Floor tape

Setup

Use the floor tape to make a line from which the students will toss. Place the hula hoops or targets on the floor next to a wall, approximately 2 feet (0.6 meter) apart.

Activity

1. Toss the ring or beanbag to the target. Toss with your right hand while stepping forward with your right foot. Repeat until the music stops.
2. Do the same with your left hand and left foot.

Skill Check

- Make sure that the student isolates one side by stepping and throwing with the hand and foot on that side.
- If using rings, make sure that the student tosses as follows:
  - Stand facing the target.
  - Hold the ring with your index (pointer) finger on the outside rim, your other three fingers on the bottom side, and your thumb on top side.
  - Throw the ring with a flick of the wrist.
  - Step toward the target with the foot on the same side as your throwing hand.
- If using beanbags, make sure that the student tosses as follows:
  - Face the target.
  - Step with the foot on the same side as your throwing hand.
  - Bring your arm back, then swing it forward and release the beanbag.

UNILATERAL ACTIVITIES

Skills Developed
Laterality, locomotor skills, motor planning

Equipment
- Jump ropes or floor tape
- Active learning cards (uppercase letters)

Setup
Using jump ropes or tape on the floor, create a series of lines in a pattern similar to that of spokes on a wheel (see diagram). Place active learning cards (in any order) in each space between the lines.

Activity
Hop over the lines, taking off and landing with the same foot. On each landing, say the letter or picture shown on the card. Go around once and then repeat with your other foot. If your teacher asks you to, change directions.

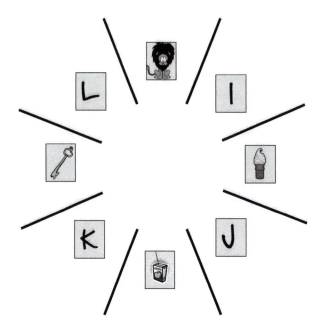

Skill Check
Make sure that the student uses proper hopping form:
- Swing your non-weight-bearing leg like a pendulum to produce power.
- On landing, keep the foot of your non-weight-bearing leg behind your body.
- Bend your arms and swing them forward to produce power.

Skills Developed

Laterality, dynamic balance, directionality

Equipment

- Floor beam
- Beanbag

Activity

1. While holding a beanbag on the back of your right hand, stand sideways on the beam and slide to the right. Slide your right foot out until your feet are shoulder width apart, then slide your left foot to catch up. Each time you move, say "right." When you reach the end of the beam, stay on the beam and switch the beanbag to your left hand.

2. While holding a beanbag on the back of your left hand, stand sideways on the beam and slide to the left. Slide your left foot out until your feet are shoulder width apart, then slide your right foot to catch up. Each time you move, say "left."

(This activity is the same as the one for week 2, station 7, except that it involves a different way of holding the beanbag.)

Skill Check

- Make sure that the student says the relevant direction (left or right) and holds the beanbag on the corresponding hand.
- Make sure that the student uses proper sliding form:
  - Turn your body sideways (shoulders aligned with the beam, toes pointed perpendicular to the beam).
  - Step sideways with your leading foot, then slide your trailing foot to meet it.
  - Move with a rhythmic continual motion.
- Make sure that the student uses dynamic balance to maintain equilibrium while in motion. He or she may need assistance due to the challenge of holding the beanbags.
- The student should do the task smoothly, without falling or having to hold on to an object (e.g., chair or wall).

Skills Developed

Locomotor skills, motor planning

Equipment

- Six cones
- Six cone collars
- Active learning cards (uppercase letters with pictures)

Setup

Place six cones approximately 4 feet (1.2 meters) apart in a straight line. Place matching letter and picture cards in the cones, alternating with each cone—for example, letter A, apple picture, letter B, ball picture.

Activity

Hop from cone to cone. At each cone, say the letter or picture shown on the card for that cone. Repeat the activity using your other foot. (This activity is the same as the one for week 5, station 1 except that it uses different active learning cards.)

Skill Check

Make sure that the student uses proper hopping form:

- Swing your non-weight-bearing leg like a pendulum to produce power.
- On landing, keep the foot of your non-weight-bearing leg behind your body.
- Bend your arms and swing them forward to produce power.

Skills Developed

Laterality, locomotor skills, spatial awareness, motor planning

Equipment

- Hopscotch mat
- Active learning cards (uppercase letters with pictures)

Activity

Double-hop sideways (i.e., hop twice in each square) through the mat using only your right foot. In each square, say what is shown on the card for the square you are hopping in. Repeat the activity using only your left foot.

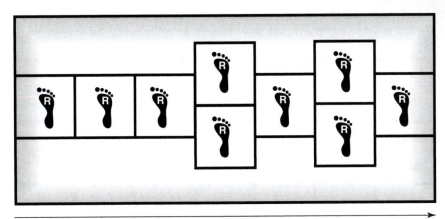

Hop 2 times in each square

Skill Check

Make sure that the student uses proper hopping form:

- Swing your non-weight-bearing leg like a pendulum to produce power.
- On landing, keep the foot of your non-weight-bearing leg behind your body.
- Bend your arms and swing them forward to produce power.

Skills Developed

Laterality, dynamic balance

Equipment

- Floor mat
- Wall mat
- Active learning cards (uppercase letters with pictures)

Activity

- Floor mat: Stand with both feet in one square and place your left hand on your left knee and your right hand on your right knee. Maintain this position as you walk heavily through the squares—first forward, then go back to the beginning and repeat the activity walking backward. As you walk, step with each foot in its own square. For each square you step in, say what is shown on the corresponding card.

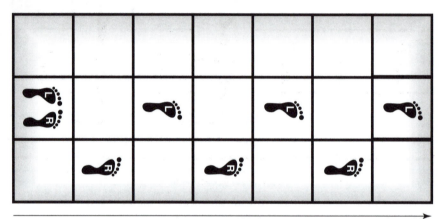

Left hand on left knee, right hand on right knee

- Wall mat: Starting with the upper left square, use one hand to touch each square on the top row of the mat. As you go from square to square, alternate touching with your index finger and with your fist. Each time you touch a square, say what is shown on the corresponding card. When you reach the end of the top row, move down to the bottom right corner of the mat, switch hands, and work back across the mat in the same manner.

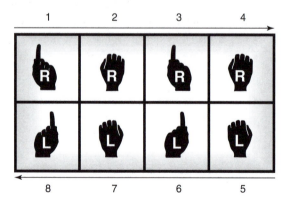

Skill Check

Make sure that students' hands are on their knees when going through the mat and that they are alternating from a fist to the index finger on each square of the wall mat.

Skills Developed

Spatial awareness, gross motor coordination

Equipment

- A 25.6-inch (65-centimeter) exercise ball
- Active learning cards (uppercase letters with pictures)
- Floor tape

Setup

Post a letter card and a picture card side by side on the wall against which students will roll the ball. The name of whatever is shown on the picture card should start with the letter shown on the letter card. Use the floor tape to mark a line 6 feet (2 meters) from the wall so that students will know where to stand to roll the ball.

Activity

1. Roll the ball to the wall with your dominant hand; be sure you step forward with the same foot as the hand you used to roll the ball (i.e., right foot and right hand or left foot and left hand). While it rebounds off the wall, say the letter shown on the card posted on the wall. Catch the ball on the rebound.

2. Roll the ball to the wall with your nondominant hand. While it rebounds off the wall, say the picture shown on the card posted on the wall. Catch the ball on the rebound and then repeat steps 1 and 2 until the music stops.

Skill Check

Make sure that the student uses proper form for unilateral rolling:

- Face your target.
- Step toward the target with the foot on the same side as your rolling arm.
- Use a pendulum motion with your arm to roll the ball (as in bowling).
- Bend your knees to lower your body and release the ball close to the ground.
- Follow through with your rolling hand toward the sky or ceiling.

Skills Developed

Laterality, motor planning, dynamic balance

Equipment

- Ladder mat
- Active learning cards (uppercase letters with pictures)

Activity

Leading with your right foot, step on the rungs of the ladder. As you step over each square, say what is shown on the card for that square. When you reach the end of the ladder, go back through the ladder with your left foot leading.

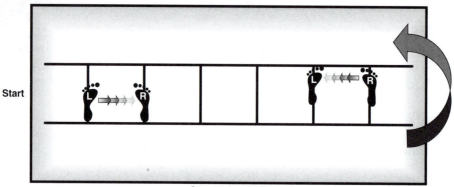

**Step to the right,
then step back to the left**

Skill Check

Make sure students are stepping with the same foot forward each time down the ladder and saying what is on the active learning card.

Skills Developed

Laterality, eye–hand coordination

Equipment

Juggling scarves

Activity

1. Toss the scarf up into the air with your right hand, then catch it with your right hand using the lion's claw catch. As you toss the scarf, say "toss up." As you catch it, say "catch down."

2. Do the same with your left hand. Repeat steps 1 and 2 until the music stops.

Skill Check

- Make sure that the student tosses and catches with the same hand.
- Make sure that the student uses proper form for the lion's claw catch:
  - Prepare by extending your hand in front of your body with your elbow bent and your palm facing outward.
  - Reach for the object by moving your hand downward with the palm facing down.
  - Catch the scarf with your hand only—not against your leg or thigh.
  - While catching, keep your eyes are on the scarf.
- Emphasize safety: The scarf is very slippery when it is on the floor. Instruct the student to keep the scarf off of the floor.

Skills Developed

Balance

Equipment

8.5-inch (22-centimeter) playground ball

Activity

1. Put your belly on the ball and try to balance yourself without touching the floor.
2. Put your belly on the ball, lift your right arm and right leg, and try to balance yourself on the ball.
3. Put your belly on the ball, lift your left arm and left leg, and try to balance yourself on the ball.

Skill Check

The student is trying to achieve static balance. Encourage him or her to make no movement if possible.

Skills Developed

Laterality, dynamic balance, directionality

Equipment

- Floor beam
- One 28-inch (0.7-meter) hoop
- Hoop stand

Setup

Place the hoop in the hoop stand and then arrange the beam so that it goes through the upright hoop.

Activity

1. Stand sideways on the beam and slide to the right. Slide your right foot out until your feet are shoulder width apart, then slide your left foot to catch up. As you go through the hoop, say "under."

2. Stand sideways on the beam and slide to the left back to where you started. Slide your left foot out until your feet are shoulder width apart, then slide your right foot to catch up. As you go through the hoop, say "under."

Skill Check

- Make sure that the student uses proper sliding form:
  - Turn your body sideways (shoulders aligned with the beam, toes pointed perpendicular to the beam).
  - Step sideways with your leading foot, then slide your trailing foot to meet it.
- Make sure that the student uses dynamic balance to maintain equilibrium while in motion. He or she may need assistance due to the challenge of holding the beanbags.
- The student should do the task smoothly, without falling or having to hold on to an object (e.g., chair or wall).

Skills Developed

Locomotor skills, motor planning

Equipment

- Six cones
- Six cone collars
- Active learning cards (uppercase letters with pictures)

Setup

Place six cones approximately 2 feet (0.6 meter) apart in a straight line. Place matching letter and picture cards in the cones, alternating with each cone—for example, letter A, apple picture, letter B, ball picture.

Activity

Hop from cone to cone. At each cone, say the letter or picture shown on the card for that cone. (This activity is the same as the one for station 1 in weeks 5 and 6.)

Skill Check

Make sure that the student uses proper hopping form:

- Swing your non-weight-bearing leg like a pendulum to produce power.
- On landing, keep the foot of your non-weight-bearing leg behind your body.
- Bend your arms and swing them forward to produce power.

Skills Developed

Laterality, locomotor skills, motor planning, spatial awareness

Equipment

- Hopscotch mat
- Beanbags
- Active learning cards (lowercase letters and spelling words)

Activity

Hop from square to square on your right foot. At each square, say what is shown on the card. At the double squares, stand on both feet and toss the beanbag up with your right hand (and catch it with your right hand) five times. When you have hopped through the mat on your right foot, return to the beginning and repeat with your left foot.

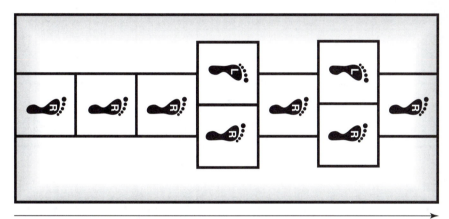

On the double squares, toss and catch a beanbag with the right hand 5 times

Skill Check

- Make sure that the student uses the correct hand for tossing and catching.
- Make sure that the student uses proper hopping form:
  - Swing your non-weight-bearing leg like a pendulum to produce power.
  - On landing, keep the foot of your non-weight-bearing leg behind your body.
  - Bend your arms and swing them forward to produce power.

Skills Developed

Laterality, dynamic balance

Equipment

- Floor mat
- Wall mat
- Juggling scarves
- Active learning cards (lowercase letters and spelling words)

Activity

- Floor mat: Step through the center lane of the mat one square at a time. In each square, stop to toss and catch a juggling scarf (to the right in the first square, to the left in the next square, and so on). While tossing and catching the scarf, say what is shown on the card for the square you are standing in.

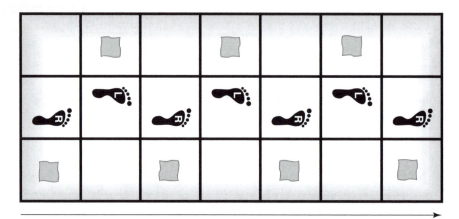

- Wall mat: Toss a scarf with one hand. While it is in the air, touch the top left square of the mat with the same hand, then catch the scarf (again with the same hand). As you toss and catch the scarf, say what is shown on the card for the current square. Continue in this manner across the top row of the mat. When you finish the top row, work back across the mat in the same manner but using your other hand and touching the squares on the bottom row.

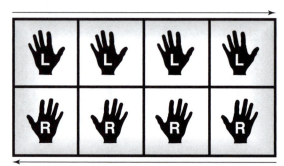

Toss scarf and touch

Skill Check

- Encourage the student to say aloud what is shown on the active learning cards.
- Make sure that the student tosses and catches the scarf with the same hand.
- For the wall mat, make sure that the student touches the mat with the tossing hand.
- Emphasize safety: The scarf is very slippery when it is on the floor. Instruct the student to keep the scarf off of the floor.

Skills Developed

Spatial awareness, gross motor coordination

Equipment

- One 25.6-inch (65-centimeter) exercise ball
- Floor tape

Setup

Use the floor tape to mark a line 6 feet (2 meters) away from the wall.

Activity

1. Roll the ball to the wall with your dominant hand, stepping with the same foot as your hand, and let it rebound off the wall. Catch the ball as it rebounds.
2. Roll the ball to the wall with your nondominant hand, stepping with the same foot as your hand, and let it rebound off the wall. Catch it as it rebounds and repeat steps 1 and 2 until the music stops.

Skill Check

Make sure that the student uses proper form for unilateral rolling:

- Face your target.
- Step toward the target with the foot on the same side as your rolling arm.
- Bend your knees to lower your body.
- Follow through with your rolling hand toward the sky or ceiling.

Skills Developed
Laterality, motor planning, dynamic balance

Equipment
- Ladder mat
- Poly spots
- Active learning cards (lowercase letters and spelling words)

Setup
Place a poly spot in every other square of the ladder mat and an active learning card in each of the remaining squares.

Activity
Hop through the squares of the mat by hopping over the poly spots and on to squares with active learning cards in them. On landing, say what is shown on the cards. When you have hopped through the mat, return to the beginning and repeat with your other foot.

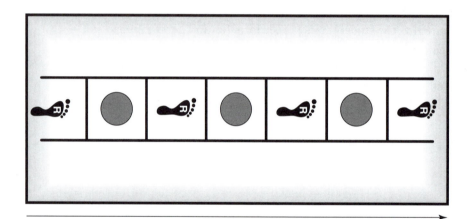

Skill Check
- Make sure that the student takes off and lands with the same foot.
- Make sure that the student uses proper hopping form:
  - Swing your non-weight-bearing leg like a pendulum to produce power.
  - On landing, keep the foot of your non-weight-bearing leg behind your body.
  - Bend your arms and swing them forward to produce power.

Skills Developed

Eye–hand coordination, laterality, manipulative skills, motor planning

Equipment

Juggling scarves

Activity

1. Toss the scarf up into the air with your right hand, then catch it with your right hand. As you toss and catch, say the ABCs or count by 10s. Do the same with your left hand.

2. Toss the scarf with one hand to a partner who catches it one hand (same side) using a lion's claw catch. Repeat until the music stops.

Skill Check

- In part 1, make sure that the student tosses and catches with the same hand.
- In both parts, make sure that the student uses proper form for the lion's claw catch:
  - Prepare by extending your hand in front of your body with your elbow bent and your palm facing outward.
  - Reach for the object by moving your hand downward with the palm facing down.
  - Catch the scarf with your hand only—not against your leg or thigh.
  - While catching, keep your eyes on the scarf.
- Emphasize safety: The scarf is very slippery when it is on the floor. Instruct the student to keep the scarf off of the floor.

Skills Developed

Laterality, spatial awareness, balance

Equipment

- One target for each student (e.g., hoops, baskets, buckets)
- One beanbag for each student
- One tennis ball for each student
- Floor tape

Setup

Mark a tape line 6 feet (2 meters) from the target.

Activity

1. Use the nondominant side of your body to throw a beanbag overhand at the target. Repeat with the dominant side of your body.

2. Use the nondominant side of your body to throw a tennis ball overhand against the wall and catch it (with or without a bounce). Repeat with the dominant side of your body.

Skill Check

- Make sure that the student uses only one hand.
- Make sure that the student uses proper form for the overhand throw:
  - The throwing motion begins with a downward movement of the throwing hand.
  - The hip and shoulders rotate so that the non-throwing side faces the wall.
  - Weight is transferred by stepping with the foot opposite the throwing hand.
  - Follow through beyond the ball and release diagonally across the body toward the nondominant side.

Skills Developed

Eye–hand coordination

Equipment

Catch-a-cup

Activity

1. Swing the ball with your right hand and try to catch it in the cup. Count aloud how many times you catch the ball.

2. Repeat with your left hand.

(This activity is the same as the one for week 4, station 4.)

Skill Check

Make sure that the student uses only one hand at a time and keeps count of how many times he or she catches the ball.

Skills Developed

Locomotor skills, motor planning

Equipment

- Six cones
- Six cone collars
- Active learning cards (uppercase letters with pictures)

Setup

Place six cones approximately 4 feet (1.2 meters) apart in a straight line. Place matching letter and picture cards in the cones, alternating with each cone—for example, letter A, apple picture, letter B, ball picture.

Activity

Hop from cone to cone. At each cone, say the letter or picture shown on the card for that cone. (This activity is the same as the one for station 1 in weeks 5, 6, and 7.)

Skill Check

Make sure that the student uses proper hopping form:

- Swing your non-weight-bearing leg like a pendulum to produce power.
- On landing, keep the foot of your non-weight-bearing leg behind your body.
- Bend your arms and swing them forward to produce power.

Skills Developed

Laterality, locomotor skills, motor planning, spatial awareness

Equipment

- Hopscotch mat
- Beanbags
- Active learning cards (uppercase letters and spelling words)

Activity

Hop from square to square on your left foot. At each square, say what is shown on the card. At the double squares, stand on both feet and toss the beanbag up with your left hand (and catch it with your left hand) five times. Once you have hopped through the mat, return to the beginning and start over with your right foot and right hand. (This activity is the same as the one for station 2 in week 7.)

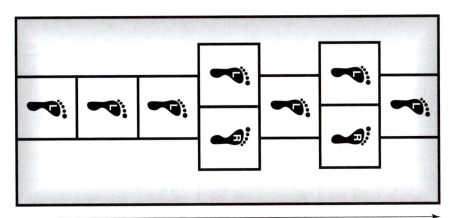

On the double square, toss and catch a beanbag with the left hand 5 times

Skill Check

- Make sure that the student uses the correct hand for tossing and catching.
- Make sure that the student uses proper hopping form:
  - Swing your non-weight-bearing leg like a pendulum to produce power.
  - On landing, keep the foot of your non-weight-bearing leg behind your body.
  - Bend your arms and swing them forward to produce power.

Skills Developed

Laterality, dynamic balance

Equipment

- Floor mat
- Wall mat
- Active learning cards (uppercase letters and spelling words)

Setup

Place one card in each middle square of the mat for partners to say together.

Activity

- Floor mat: Step sideways from square to square along one edge of the mat while a partner does the same along the opposite edge of the mat (face each other). As you step through the squares, use one hand to roll the ball slowly back and forth with your partner (one roll per square). For each square you step in, say what is shown on the corresponding card. When you reach the end of the mat, go back to the beginning and repeat until the music stops.

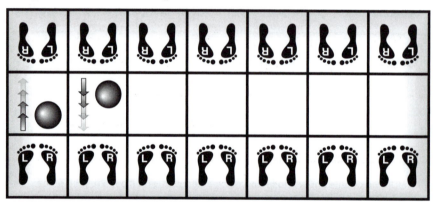

- Wall mat: Starting with the top left square of the wall mat, touch an elbow to each square in the top row. As you touch each square, say what is shown on the card for that square. When finished with the top row, move to the bottom row, switch to your other elbow, and work your way back across the mat in the same way.

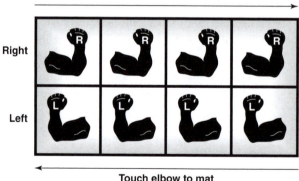

Touch elbow to mat

Skill Check

Make sure that the student uses proper form for unilateral rolling:

- Face your target. Step with your same-side foot toward the target (e.g., if rolling with your right hand, step with your right foot). Use a pendulum motion with your arm to roll the ball (as in bowling).
- Bend your knees to lower your body and release the ball close to the ground. Follow through with your rolling hand toward the sky or ceiling.

Skills Developed

Laterality, motor planning, gross motor coordination

Equipment

- One stomp board for each student
- One beanbag for each student
- Short-handled racket (e.g., a ping-pong paddle)

Activity

1. Hold the racket in your right hand and stomp the board with your right foot to project the beanbag into the air. Hit the beanbag with the racket. Retrieve the beanbag and repeat until the music stops.
2. Do the same activity but stomp with your left foot and hold the racket in your left hand.

Skill Check

- Caution the student to neither run and stomp nor jump and stomp because the board may slide causing the student to slip and fall. Also the movement is more controlled when the stomp is not accompanied with a run or jump.
- Make sure that the student uses the same side of the body to stomp and hold the paddle (e.g., stomp with right foot, hold racket in right hand).

Skills Developed

Laterality, dynamic balance

Equipment

- Ladder mat
- Active learning cards (uppercase letters and spelling words)

Activity

Gallop through the squares by stepping on the rungs with your right foot leading and your right hand touching your right thigh. As you cross each square, say what is shown on the card for that square. When finished, go to the beginning and gallop through the ladder with your left foot leading and your left hand touching your left thigh.

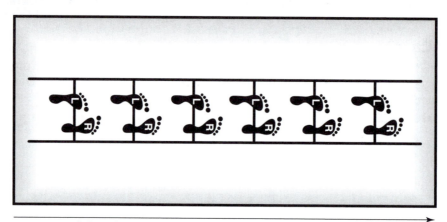

Gallop with the right hand on right leg, then left hand on left leg

Skill Check

Make sure that the student uses proper form for galloping:

- To begin, flex your arms and hold them at waist level.
- Take a starting stance with one foot in front of the other. Step forward with your front foot, then bring your back foot next to or just behind your lead foot.
- Next comes a brief period when both of your feet are off the floor.
- Move your feet with a rhythmic pattern.

Skills Developed

Eye–hand coordination, gross motor development

Equipment

One beanbag per student

Activity

1. Toss and catch the beanbag five times with your right hand (palm up).
2. Toss and catch the beanbag five times with your left hand (palm up).
3. Toss the beanbag with your right hand (palm up) and catch it five times with your right hand (palm down).
4. Toss the beanbag with your left hand (palm up) and catch the beanbag five times with your left hand (palm down).

Skill Check

- For parts 1 and 2 (palm up), make sure the student uses a one-hand bird's nest catch:
  - Prepare by extending your catching hand in front of your body with your elbow bent.
  - As the beanbag approaches, reach for it with your palm up.
  - Catch the beanbag with your hand only—not against your chest.
  - Keep your eyes on the beanbag while catching it.
- For parts 3 and 4 (palm down), make sure the student uses a lion's claw catch:
  - Prepare by extending your catching hand in front of your body with your elbow bent and your palm facing outward.
  - Reach for the beanbag by moving your hand downward with the palm facing down.
  - Catch the beanbag with your hand only—not against your leg or thigh.
  - While catching, keep your eyes on the beanbag.

Skills Developed

Directionality, laterality, dynamic balance

Equipment

- Floor beam
- One 28-inch (0.7-meter) hoop
- Hoop stand
- Two cones
- Foam hurdle that can be supported by two cones

Setup

Place the hoop in the hoop stand and arrange the beam so that it goes through the hoop. Then place the hurdle so that it goes over the beam. As an alternative, put a tape line on the floor instead of using a floor beam.

Activity

1. Stand sideways on the beam and slide to the right along the beam. Go sideways through the hoop that is positioned over the beam. Step sideways over the hurdle that is positioned over the beam.

2. Then go back to the beginning of the beam and start over. Face the other direction so that you slide to the left along the beam.

Skill Check

- Make sure that the student uses proper sliding form:
  - Turn your body sideways (shoulders aligned with the beam, toes pointed perpendicular to the beam).
  - Step sideways with your leading foot, then slide your trailing foot to meet it.
- Make sure that the student uses dynamic balance to maintain equilibrium while in motion. He or she may need assistance due to the challenge of holding the beanbags.
- The student should do the task smoothly, without falling or having to hold on to an object (e.g., chair or wall).

Skills Developed

Eye–hand coordination, gross motor development

Equipment

- One beanbag for each student
- One bucket for each student
- Floor tape

Setup

Use the floor tape to mark a line 6 feet (2 meters) from the targets.

Activity

1. Toss a beanbag underhand into the bucket with your right hand. Be sure to step with your same-side foot as you toss. Try 10 times and count each toss aloud.
2. Repeat using your left hand and left foot.
3. Toss a beanbag underhand into the bucket with your right hand. Be sure to step with your same-side foot as you toss. Try seven times and say aloud a day of the week with each toss.
4. Repeat using your left hand.

Skill Check

- Make sure that the student isolates one side of the body by taking a step with the same-side foot as they toss.
- Make sure that the student uses proper form for an underhand toss:
  - Face the target. Step with the foot on the same side as your throwing hand. Bring your arm back, then swing it forward and release the beanbag.

CROSS-LATERAL ACTIVITIES

Cross-lateral activities involve the hand and foot crossing the vertical midline of the body. When a child can cross the vertical midline of the body with his or her hands and feet, this aids in moving from the left side of the page to the right side during reading by activating or re-establishing communication between both sides of the brain.

Use the following guide to choosing the appropriate active learning cards for each week:

Week 1: Colors and shapes

Week 2: Numbers

Week 3: Lowercase letters

Week 4: Lowercase letters with pictures

Week 5: Uppercase letters

Week 6: Uppercase letters with pictures

Week 7: Lowercase letters and spelling words

Week 8: Uppercase letters and spelling words

Although these categories give you general guidelines to go by, some specific activities might call for a different category than described here.

Skills Developed

Locomotor skills, motor planning, spatial awareness

Equipment

- Six cones
- Active learning cards (colors and shapes)

Setup

Place six cones 4 feet (1.2 meters) apart in a straight line.

Activity

Crawl from cone to cone. Along the way, touch each cone and say the letter or shape shown on the card for that cone.

Skill Check

Make sure that the student uses proper crawling form:

- Raise your torso and support your weight on your hands and knees with your stomach off the floor.
- Move without stopping.
- Your right hand and left knee (and your left hand and right knee) should move forward simultaneously.

Skills Developed

Laterality, locomotor skills, motor planning

Equipment

- Hopscotch mat
- Beanbag
- Active learning cards (colors and shapes)

Activity

Hop from square to square on your left foot while carrying a beanbag in your right hand. On landing in each square, say what is shown on the card for that square.

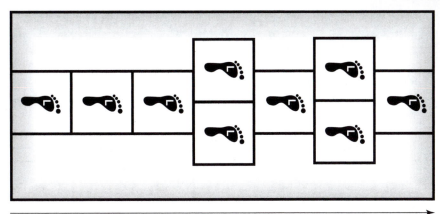

Hop on the left foot; carry a beanbag in the right hand

Skill Check

Make sure that the student uses proper hopping form:

- Swing your non-weight-bearing leg like a pendulum to produce power.
- On landing, keep the foot of your non-weight-bearing leg behind your body.
- Bend your arms and swing them forward to produce power.

Skills Developed

Laterality, motor planning, gross motor coordination

Equipment

- Floor mat
- Wall mat
- Active learning cards (colors and shapes)

Setup

If you make two sets of the cards, you may use the same card in paired squares. If you only have one set of cards, go ahead and put different cards in each square.

Activity

- Floor mat: Starting with both feet in the first middle square, walk forward from square to square in a crossover pattern. On each step with your right foot, place it in the next square to the left. On each step with your left foot, place it in the next square to the right. Continue this pattern to the end of the mat. For each step, say what is shown on the card for that square.

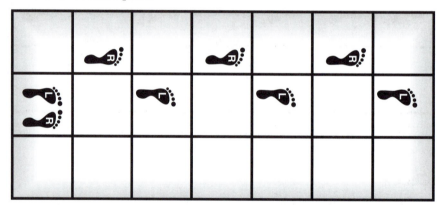

- Wall mat: Start at the top left corner of the mat. Reach out and cross your arms in front of you to touch a pair of squares on the wall mat (each hand in its own square). Your right hand should be in the left square of the pair, and your left hand should be in the right square of the pair. Each time you touch, say what is shown on the cards for the squares you are touching. Move left to right across the top row of squares and then continue moving right to left across the bottom row of squares.

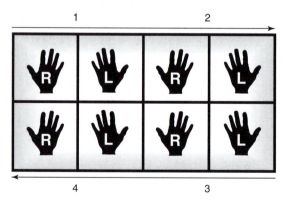

Skill Check

- Encourage the student to speak loudly when saying what is shown on the shape card.
- Encourage the student to watch foot placement. The left foot should be on the right side of the midline of the body and the right foot should be on the left side of the midline of the body.

Skills Developed

Cross-lateral awareness, gross motor planning

Equipment

- Tumbling mat
- Active learning cards (colors and shapes)

Setup

Place five cards on the floor beside the tumbling mat.

Activity

Belly-crawl the length of the mat. As you pass each card beside the mat, say the color and shape that it shows.

Skill Check

Make sure the student uses proper form for belly crawling:

- Keep your stomach on the floor.
- Move without stopping.
- Your right hand and left knee (and your left hand and right knee) should move forward simultaneously.

CROSS-LATERAL ACTIVITIES

Skills Developed

Dynamic balance, motor planning, gross motor coordination

Equipment

- Ladder mat
- Active learning cards (colors and shapes)

Activity

Walk through the ladder mat, stepping on each rung with emphasis on moving your arms in opposition: Move your left arm simultaneously with your right leg, and move your right arm with your left leg. As you walk through each square, say what is shown on the card for that square.

Skill Check

- Encourage the students to say aloud the colors and shapes shown on each card.
- Watch for balance issues and provide support (an arm for students to hold on to) where needed.
    - Make sure that the student uses dynamic balance to maintain equilibrium while in motion.
    - The student should do the task smoothly, without falling or having to hold on to an object (e.g., chair or wall).
- Make sure that the student uses proper form for walking:
    - Stand tall by keeping your body erect.
    - You should be able to draw a straight line from ear to shoulder.
    - Align your hips, knees, and ankles.
    - Your head should be level and looking forward, and your chin should be parallel to the ground.
    - Your shoulders should be relaxed and your arms bent.
    - Swing your arms in opposition to your foot movement.
    - Walk heel to toe.

Skills Developed

Laterality, motor planning, gross motor coordination

Equipment

- Seven poly spots of various colors
- Active learning cards (colors and shapes)

Setup

Place the poly spots in a pattern of your choice, making sure they are 2 feet (about half a meter) apart. Beside each poly spot, place an active learning card.

Activity

Alternate left foot and right foot when leaping from poly spot to poly spot. Move your arms in opposition to your feet: When leaping with your left foot, bring your right arm forward. When leaping with your right foot, bring your left arm forward. For each poly spot, say the color and shape shown on the card and the color of the poly spot.

Skill Check

Make sure that the student uses proper form for leaping:

- Move continuously without hesitation before the leap.
- Take off on one foot and land on the other.
- Use a long stride (longer than in running) in which both feet are off the ground during each leap.
- For each leap, reach in front of your body with the arm on the opposite side from your leading (leaping) foot.

Skills Developed

Walking, dynamic balance, grapevine

Equipment

Floor beam

Activity

1. Say the alphabet as you walk forward on the floor beam.

2. Go back to the starting point and say the alphabet as you walk backward on the beam.

3. Go back to the starting point and say the alphabet as you walk sideways on the beam doing a grapevine crossover step.

Skill Check

- Watch for balance issues and provide support (an arm for the student to hold on to) when needed. If the student has difficulty with the floor beam, he or she may walk on a tape line on the floor.
  - Make sure that the student uses dynamic balance to maintain equilibrium while in motion.
  - The student should do the task smoothly, without falling or having to hold on to an object (e.g., chair or wall).
- Make sure that the student uses proper form for the grapevine step:
  - When moving to the right, step with your right foot first.
  - Follow with your left foot moving *in front of* and across your right foot.
  - Then step out again with your right foot.
  - Follow with your left foot moving *behind* your right foot.
  - Continue with this pattern.

Skills Developed

Cross-lateral awareness, dynamic balance

Equipment

- Leap, hop, and jump mat
- Active learning cards (colors and shapes)
- Floor tape

Activity

Start running from a line 10 feet (3 meters) from the mat and leap across the mat. Start at the narrow end and work your way to the wide end. Emphasize using good leaping form. On landing, say what is shown on the card for the section of the mat you are leaping over.

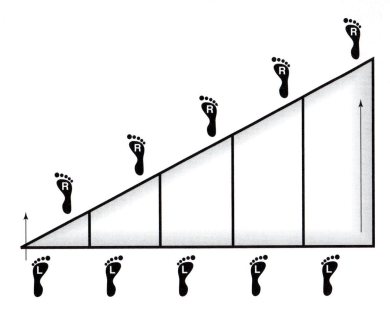

Skill Check

Make sure that the student uses proper form for leaping:

- Move continuously without hesitation before the leap.
- Take off on one foot and land on the other.
- Use a long stride (longer than in running) in which both feet are off the ground during each leap.
- For each leap, reach in front of your body with the arm on the opposite side from your leading (leaping) foot.

Skills Developed

Locomotor skills, motor planning, spatial awareness

Equipment

- Six cones
- Active learning cards (numbers)

Setup

Place six cones 4 feet (1 meter) apart in a straight line.

Activity

Crawl from cone to cone. Along the way, touch each cone and say the number shown on the card for that cone. (This activity is the same as the one for week 1, station 1 except that it uses different active learning cards.)

Skill Check

- Make sure the student uses proper crawling form:
  - Raise your torso and support your weight on your hands and knees with your stomach off the floor.
  - Move without stopping.
  - Your right hand and left knee (and your left hand and right knee) should move forward simultaneously.
- Be sure the student correctly identifies the numbers on the cards.

Skills Developed

Laterality, locomotor skills, motor planning

Equipment

- Hopscotch mat
- Beanbags
- Active learning cards (numbers)

Activity

Hop from square to square on your right foot while carrying a beanbag in your left hand. On landing in each square, say what is shown on the card for that square. (This activity is the same as the one for week 1, station 2, except that it uses the other foot.)

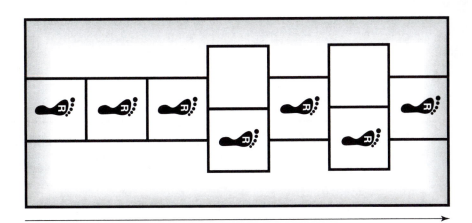

Skill Check

Make sure that the student uses proper hopping form:
- Swing your non-weight-bearing leg like a pendulum to produce power.
- On landing, keep the foot of your non-weight-bearing leg behind your body.
- Bend your arms and swing them forward to produce power.

Skills Developed
Laterality, motor planning, gross motor coordination

Equipment
- Floor mat
- Wall mat
- One set of beanbags (four beanbags in four different colors that match those of the active learning cards)
- Active learning cards (numbers)

Setup
Place the beanbags next to the station cone (four for each student).

Activity
- Floor mat: Stand side by side with a partner on the mat and hold hands. Jump forward one square with your partner, making a quarter-turn in the air so that you land face to face and holding both hands. Jump sideways to the next square with your partner, again making a quarter-turn in the air (but turning back the other way) so that you land facing forward and holding only one hand. Continue with this pattern to the end of the mat. Each time you land in a square, say what is shown on the card for that square.

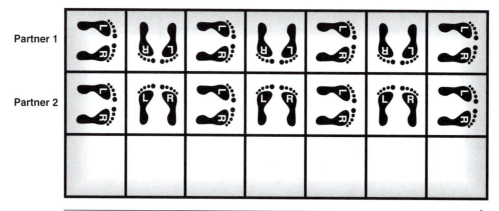

- Wall mat: Pick up a beanbag and touch it to the card on the mat that matches the beanbag in color. As you touch the card, say what is shown on the card. Do this pattern for each of the beanbags one at a time.

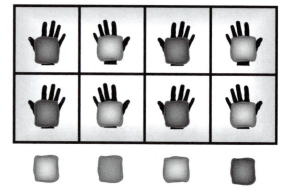

Skill Check
- Encourage the student to speak loudly in saying the numbers and colors.
- Encourage the student to match his or her foot placement to that shown in the diagram of the floor mat.
- Remind the student to focus on using the correct form for a standing long jump:
  - Bend both knees with your arms extended behind your body before takeoff.
  - When jumping, thrust your arms forcefully forward and upward (above your head).
  - Take off and land with both feet.
  - Move your arms downward on landing.

Skills Developed

Cross-laterality, directionality, balance, eye–hand coordination

Equipment

- 8.5-inch (22-centimeter) playground ball
- Floor tape

Setup

Use the floor tape to mark an 8-foot (2.4-meter) line.

Activity

Hold the ball and walk forward on the line using a crossover step: On each step with your right foot, step to the left of the line; on each step with your left foot, step to the right of the line. Continue this pattern to the end of the line. After each step, bounce the ball with either hand.

Skill Check

- Make sure that the student uses proper form for dribbling:
  - Keep your eyes up.
  - Use your finger pads—not your fingertips.
  - For good control, dribble at your side and at waist level or lower.
  - Dribble the ball in the "foot pocket" created by dropping your right foot behind your left foot (or vice versa if dribbling with your left hand).
- Make sure that students use the proper form for the crossover step:
  - Be sure that on each step with your right foot, you step to the left of the line and on each step with your left foot, you step to the right of the line.

CROSS-LATERAL ACTIVITIES

Skills Developed

Laterality, motor planning, dynamic balance

Equipment

- Ladder mat
- Active learning cards (numbers)

Activity

Do a sideways grapevine crossover step along the right side of the ladder. As you pass each square of the ladder, say what is shown on the card for that square.

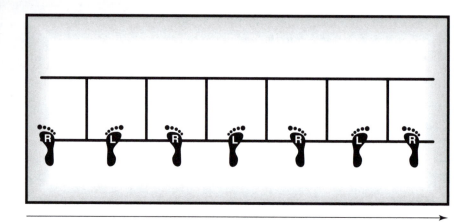

Skill Check

- Make sure the student's body is turned sideways so shoulders are aligned with the ladder on the floor.
- Make sure that the student uses proper form for the grapevine step:
  - When moving to the right, step with your right foot first.
  - Follow with your left foot moving *in front of* and across your right foot.
  - Then step out again with your right foot.
  - Follow with your left foot moving *behind* your right foot.
  - Continue with this pattern.

Skills Developed

Eye–hand coordination, gross motor development

Equipment

- One stomp board for each student
- One beanbag for each student

Activity

1. Stomp on the board with your right foot to launch the beanbag into the air. Catch the beanbag with your left hand. Make 10 tries and keep count by speaking out loud.
2. Repeat the activity but this time stomp with your left foot and catch with your right hand.
3. Stomp on the board with your right foot to launch the beanbag. While the beanbag is in the air, clap once, then catch it with your left hand. Make 10 tries and keep count out loud.
4. Repeat the activity but this time stomp with your right foot and catch with your left hand.

Skill Check

- Make sure that the student uses proper form for cross-lateral stomping:
  - Face the board with your feet slightly apart and adjacent to each other.
  - Step quickly on the stomp board with minimum force (not too hard).
  - If stomping with your right foot, catch with your left hand; if stomping with your left foot, catch with your right hand.
- Make sure that the student uses proper form for catching:
  - Prepare by extending your hand in front of your body with your elbows bent.
  - Reach for the object as it approaches you.
  - Catch the object with one hand only—not against your chest.
  - Give with object as it lands in your hand (bring it in toward your body).
  - Keep your eyes on the object.

Skills Developed

Dynamic balance, spatial awareness

Equipment

- Floor beam
- Hoop with stand
- Two cones with hurdle

Activity

Walk forward on the beam from one end to the other. Along the way, step over the hurdle and through the hoop.

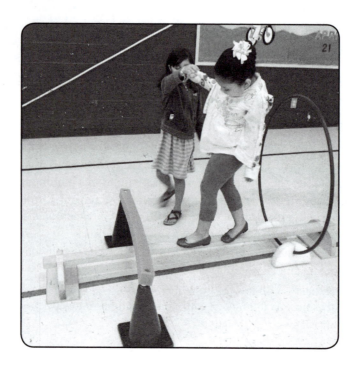

Skill Check

- Watch for balance issues and provide support (an arm for the student to hold on to) when needed. If the student has difficulty with the floor beam, he or she may walk on a tape line on the floor.
- Make sure that the student uses dynamic balance to maintain equilibrium while in motion.
- The student should do the task smoothly, without falling or having to hold on to an object (e.g., chair or wall).

Skills Developed

Cross-lateral awareness, dynamic balance

Equipment

- Leap, hop, and jump mat
- Active learning cards (numbers)
- Floor tape

Activity

Start running at a line 10 feet (3 meters) from the mat and leap across the mat. Start at the narrow end and work your way to the wide end. Emphasize using good leaping form. On landing, say what is shown on the card for the section of the mat you are leaping over. (This activity is the same as the one for week 1, station 8 except that it uses different active learning cards.)

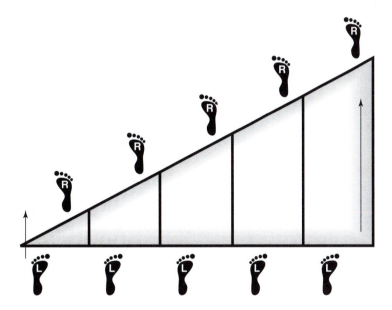

Skill Check

Make sure that the student uses proper form for leaping:

- Move continuously without hesitation before the leap.
- Take off on one foot and land on the other.
- Use a long stride (longer than in running) in which both feet are off the ground during each leap.
- For each leap, reach in front of your body with the arm on the opposite side from your leading (leaping) foot.

Skills Developed

Locomotor skills, motor planning, spatial awareness

Equipment

- Six cones
- Active learning cards (lowercase letters)

Setup

Place six cones 4 feet (1.2 meters) apart in a straight line.

Activity

Crawl from cone to cone. Along the way, touch each cone and say the number shown on the card for that cone. (This activity is the same as the one for station 1 in weeks 1 and 2 except that it uses different active learning cards.)

Skill Check

Make sure the student uses proper crawling form:

- Raise your torso and support your weight on your hands and knees with your stomach off the floor.
- Move without stopping.
- Your right hand and left knee (and your left hand and right knee) should move forward simultaneously.

Skills Developed

Laterality, locomotor skills, motor planning

Equipment

- Hopscotch mat
- Active learning cards (lowercase letters)

Activity

March (doing high-knees) from square to square, saying what is shown on the card for each square you step into. When stepping with your left foot, place your right hand on your left knee; when stepping with your right foot, place your left hand on your right knee. At the double (side-by-side) square locations, cross your feet (stepping into the left square with your right foot and into the right square with your left foot).

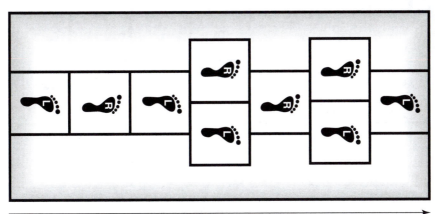

Touch your knee with your opposite hand

Skill Check

Make sure that student places his or her feet as shown on the diagram so that on double (side-by-side) squares they cross feet.

Skills Developed

Laterality, motor planning, gross motor coordination

Equipment

- Floor mat
- Wall mat
- Active learning cards (lowercase letters)

Activity

- Floor mat: Stand with your legs crossed and your feet side by side in the first middle square. Jump forward and uncross your legs before landing in the next square. Jump forward again, recrossing your legs before landing in the next square. Proceed through the squares in this pattern, saying what is shown on each card as you get to it.

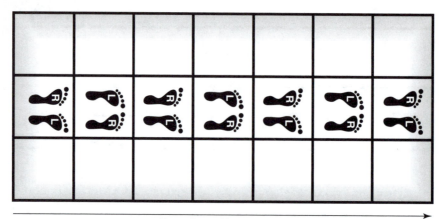

Cross feet with each jump

- Wall mat: In this activity, use the center four squares of the mat. Stand in front of the wall mat. Clap once and touch your right hand to the upper left square of the center four while saying what is shown on the card for that square. Clap again and touch your left hand to the upper right square of the center four while saying what is shown on that card. Clap again and touch your right hand to the bottom left square of the center four while saying what is shown on the card. Clap again and touch your left hand to the bottom right square of the center four while saying what is shown on that card.

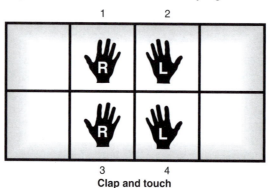

Clap and touch

Skill Check

- Encourage the student to say aloud the letter on each card.
- Encourage the student to take care with his or her foot placement. Make sure that legs are crossed when directions require them to be and uncrossed when they are supposed to be uncrossed.

Skills Developed

Cross-lateral awareness

Equipment

- 8.5-inch (22-centimeter) playground ball
- Foam brick
- Two cones
- Floor tape

Setup

Position two cones 5 feet (1.5 meters) apart. Use the floor tape to mark a line 10 feet (3 meters) from where students will be kicking the ball in step 2.

Activity

Taking a 10-foot (3-meter) approach, run up to the ball without slowing and use your right foot to kick the ball at the brick between the cones. When kicking with your right foot, extend your left arm forward. Repeat with your left foot and right arm. Repeat the sequence five times for each side.

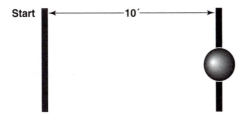 

Skill Check

Make sure that the student uses proper kicking form:

- Make a fast and nonstop approach to the ball.
- Just prior to kicking the ball, take a long stride.
- Place your nonkicking foot even with or slightly behind the ball.
- Kick the ball with the instep or toe of the preferred foot.
- Follow through by landing on your kicking foot.

171

Skills Developed

Laterality, locomotor skills, motor planning

Equipment

- Ladder mat
- Active learning cards (lowercase letters)

Activity

Walk through the ladder mat from rung to rung. During each step, touch the heel of your stepping foot to the opposite hand (i.e., right heel to left hand, left heel to right hand). Along the way, say what is shown on the card for each square as you step past it.

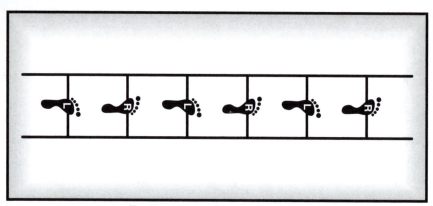

Touch your heel with your opposite hand

Skill Check

- Make sure student says aloud what is shown on the cards.
- Make sure that the student uses proper form for walking:
  - Stand tall by keeping your body erect.
  - You should be able to draw a straight line from ear to shoulder.
  - Align your hips, knees, and ankles.
  - Your head should be level and looking forward, and your chin should be parallel to the ground.
  - Your shoulders should be relaxed and your arms bent.
  - Swing your arms in opposition to your foot movement.
  - Walk heel to toe.

Skills Developed

Laterality, motor planning, gross motor coordination

Equipment

- One scooter board for each child
- Four cones
- Active learning cards (lowercase letters)

Setup

Position the cones 2 feet (about half a meter) apart in a straight line.

Activity

1. Lie on your tummy on the scooter board and push yourself from cone to cone. Alternate sides in pushing—first with your right leg and left hand, then with your left leg and right hand, and so on. As you pass each cone, say what is shown on the card.

2. Sit on the scooter board and use your feet to propel yourself from cone to cone. Alternate sides by using first your right foot, then your left foot, and so on. As you pass each cone, say what is shown on the card.

Skill Check

- Stress scooter board safety (e.g., never stand on the board, keep hands on the side, keep hair and clothing away from the wheels).
- Watch for cross-laterality (i.e., right hand used with left leg and left hand used with right leg).
- Make sure the student says aloud what is shown on the card as he or she moves past each cone.

Skills Developed

Laterality, motor planning, gross motor coordination

Equipment

- Four buckets in primary colors (red, yellow, blue, green)
- Four beanbags in primary colors (red, yellow, blue, green)

Activity

Crawl from beanbag to beanbag, putting each one in the bucket with the matching color. When picking up a beanbag from the floor, use whichever hand is closest to it, and use that same hand to put the beanbag in the bucket—do not switch hands!

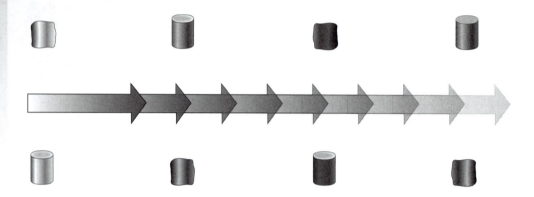

Skill Check

- Make sure that the student does not switch hands before placing the beanbag in the bucket.
- Make sure that the student uses proper crawling form:
  - Raise your torso and support your weight on your hands and knees with your stomach off the floor.
  - Move without stopping.
  - Your right hand and left knee (and your left hand and right knee) should move forward simultaneously.

Skills Developed

Cross-lateral awareness, dynamic balance

Equipment

- Leap, hop, and jump mat
- Floor tape
- Active learning cards (lowercase letters)

Activity

Start at a line 10 feet (3 meters) from the mat and leap across the mat. Start at the narrow end and work your way to the wide end. Emphasize using good leaping form. On landing, say what is shown on the card for the section of the mat you are leaping over. (This activity is the same as the one for station 8 in weeks 1 and 2 except that it uses different active learning cards.)

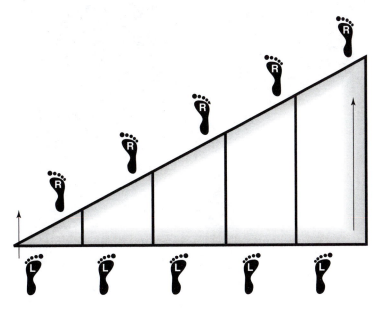

Skill Check

Make sure that the student uses proper form for leaping:

- Move continuously without hesitation before the leap.
- Take off on one foot and land on the other.
- Use a long stride (longer than in running) in which both feet are off the ground during each leap.
- For each leap, reach in front of your body with the arm on the opposite side from your leading (leaping) foot.

Skills Developed

Locomotor skills, motor planning, spatial awareness

Equipment

- Six cones
- Active learning cards (uppercase letters)

Setup

Place the cones 4 feet (1 meter) apart.

Activity

Do grapevine (crossover) steps from cone to cone. Along the way, touch each cone and say the letter shown on the card for that cone.

Skill Check

Make sure that the student uses proper form for the grapevine step:

- When moving to the right, step with your right foot first.
- Follow with your left foot moving *in front of* and across your right foot.
- Then step out again with your right foot.
- Follow with your left foot moving *behind* your right foot.
- Continue with this pattern.

Skills Developed

Laterality, locomotor skills, motor planning

Equipment

- Hopscotch mat
- 8.5-inch (22-centimeter) playground ball
- Active learning cards (lowercase letters with pictures)

Activity

Step into the first square and bounce the ball with your left hand on the right side of your body. As you bounce the ball, say what is shown on the card for the square you just stepped into. Move to the next square, bounce the ball with your right hand on the left side, and say what is shown on the current card. At the double squares, bounce the ball with your left hand on the right side and with your right hand on the left side, and say what is shown on each card.

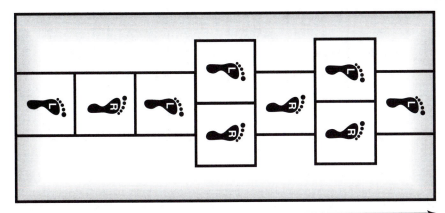

Bounce a ball with your left hand on your right side, then with your right hand on your left side

Skill Check

- Make sure the student crosses his or her midline to bounce the ball.
- Make sure that the student uses proper form for dribbling:
  - Keep your eyes up.
  - Use your finger pads—not your fingertips.
  - For good control, dribble at your side and at waist level or lower.
  - Dribble the ball in your "foot pocket" created by dropping your right foot behind your left foot (or vice versa if using left hand).
- Make sure that the student uses proper form for walking:
  - Stand tall by keeping your body erect.
  - You should be able to draw a straight line from ear to shoulder.
  - Align your hips, knees, and ankles.
  - Your head should be level and looking forward, and your chin should be parallel to the ground.
  - Your shoulders should be relaxed and your arms bent.
  - Swing your arms in opposition to your foot movement.
  - Walk heel to toe.

Skills Developed

Laterality, motor planning, gross motor coordination

Equipment

- Floor mat
- Wall mat
- Active learning cards (lowercase letters with pictures)

Activity

- Floor mat: Walk through the middle row of the mat on your heels, stepping into a new square with each foot. Along the way, say what is shown on the card for each square as you step on it.

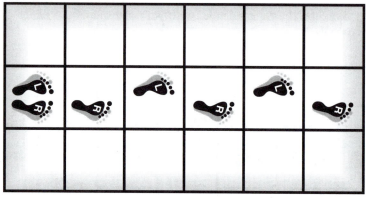

Walk on heels

- Wall mat: Use your hands to do a grapevine pattern across the mat. Place the right hand in the top box on the left side of the wall mat. Next place the left hand in the adjacent square by crossing over the right hand. Continue by moving the right hand to the next adjacent square and then the left hand. Return to the beginning of the mat and repeat, starting with your right hand in the bottom box on the left side of the wall mat and moving from left to right. Move to adjacent squares with alternating hands. Along the way, say what is shown on the card for each square as you touch it.

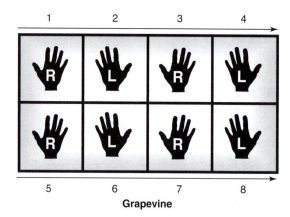

Grapevine

Skill Check

- Encourage the student to speak loudly in saying what is on each active learning card.
- Look to see that the student is walking on his or her heels.

178

Skills Developed

Cross-pattern awareness, gross motor coordination

Equipment

Long jump ropes

Setup

Use ropes to create various shapes on the floor.

Activity

1. Walk around the ropes and say aloud what shape they form. Repeat the name of the shape several times as you walk around it.

2. Jog around the ropes and say aloud what shape they form. Repeat the name of the shape several times as you jog around it.

3. Crawl around the ropes and say aloud what shape they form. Repeat the name of the shape several times as you crawl around it.

Skill Check

- For walking, make sure that the student uses proper form as follows:
  - Stand tall by keeping your body erect.
  - You should be able to draw a straight line from ear to shoulder.
  - Align your hips, knees, and ankles.
  - Your head should be level and looking forward, and your chin should be parallel to the ground.
  - Your shoulders should be relaxed and your arms bent.
  - Swing your arms in opposition to your foot movement.
  - Walk heel to toe.
- For jogging, make sure that the student uses proper form as follows:
  - Swing your arms in opposition to your foot movement.
  - Your shoulders should be relaxed and your arms bent.
  - There should be a brief period where both your feet are off the ground.
  - Land on the heel or toe of your foot (do not land flat footed).
  - Bend your trailing leg at a 90-degree angle.
- For crawling, make sure that the student uses proper form as follows:
  - Raise your torso and support your weight on your hands and knees with your stomach off the floor.
  - Move without stopping.
  - Your right hand and left knee (and your left hand and right knee) should move forward simultaneously.

Skills Developed

Laterality, locomotor skills, motor planning

Equipment

- Ladder mat
- Active learning cards (lowercase letters with pictures)

Activity

Pull your left knee up with both hands, then step with your left foot onto the first rung of the ladder. Pull your right knee up with both hands, then step with your right foot onto the next rung. Continue this pattern as you walk through the mat. For each step, say what is shown on the card for the current square.

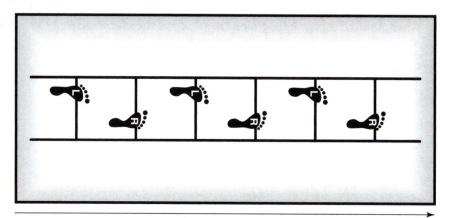

Pull your knee up with both hands

Skill Check

- Encourage the student to progress slowly and carefully.
- Make sure the student says aloud what is shown on each card.

Skills Developed

Eye–hand coordination, cross-lateral awareness

Equipment

- One stomp board for each student
- One beanbag for each student
- One 13-inch (33-centimeter) paddle for each student

Activity

1. Hold the paddle in your left hand and stomp on the board with your right foot to launch the beanbag into the air. Hit the beanbag with the paddle and say a letter of the alphabet.

2. Retrieve your beanbag and repeat the activity but this time stomp with your left foot and hold the paddle with your right hand. Hit the beanbag with the paddle and say the next letter of the alphabet. Repeat steps 1 and 2, working your way through the alphabet, until you have done each side 5 times.

Skill Check

- Make sure that the student uses proper form for cross-lateral stomping:
  - Face the board with your feet slightly apart and adjacent to each other.
  - Step quickly on the stomp board with minimum force (not too hard).
  - If stomping with your right foot, use the paddle with your left hand; if stomping with your left foot, use the paddle with your right hand.
- Caution the student to neither run and stomp nor jump and stomp because the board may slide causing the student to slip and fall. Also the movement is more controlled when the stomp is not accompanied with a run or jump.

Skills Developed

Laterality, motor planning, gross motor coordination

Equipment

Ladder mat

Activity

Bear-walk through the ladder mat while saying the alphabet.

Skill Check

- Stress moving in opposition (when the right foot moves, the left hand moves).
- Make sure that the student uses the following form for the bear walk:
  - Bend forward at your waist.
  - Place both hands on the ground.
  - Travel forward slowly.
  - Move the hand and foot on opposite sides of your body at the same time (e.g., left hand, right foot).

Skills Developed

Cross-lateral awareness, dynamic balance

Equipment

- Leap, hop, and jump mat
- Floor tape
- Active learning cards (spelling words)

Activity

Start from a line 10 feet (3 meters) from the mat and leap across the mat. Start at the narrow end and work your way to the wide end. Emphasize using good leaping form. On landing, say what is shown on the card for the section of the mat you are leaping over. (This activity is the same as the one for station 8 in weeks 1, 2, and 3 except that it uses different active learning cards.)

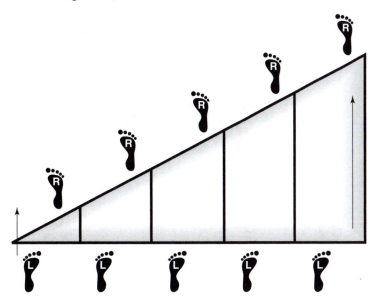

Skill Check

Make sure that the student uses proper form for leaping:

- Move continuously without hesitation before the leap.
- Take off on one foot and land on the other.
- Use a long stride (longer than in running) in which both feet are off the ground during each leap.
- For each leap, reach in front of your body with the arm on the opposite side from your leading (leaping) foot.

Skills Developed

Locomotor skills, motor planning, spatial awareness

Equipment

- Six cones
- Active learning cards (uppercase letters with pictures)

Setup

Place the cones 4 feet (1 meter) apart.

Activity

Bear-walk from cone to cone. Along the way, touch each cone and say the letter or picture shown on the card for that cone.

Skill Check

- Make sure that the student uses proper form for the bear walk:
  - Bend forward at your waist.
  - Place both hands on the ground.
  - Travel forward slowly.
  - Move the hand and foot on opposite sides of your body at the same time (e.g., left hand, right foot).
- Make sure the students say the letter shown on each card aloud.

Skills Developed

Laterality, locomotor skills, motor planning

Equipment

- Hopscotch mat
- Active learning cards (uppercase letters)

Activity

Jump from square to square, crossing or uncrossing your feet with each jump (i.e., cross on first jump, uncross on second jump, cross on third jump, and so on). With each jump, say what is shown on the active learning card for the current square.

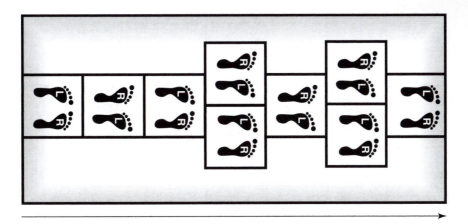

Skill Check

- Remind the student to slow down and focus on using the correct form for a standing long jump:
  - Bend both knees with your arms extended behind your body before takeoff.
  - When jumping, thrust your arms forcefully forward and upward (above your head).
  - Take off and land with both feet.
  - Move your arms downward on landing.
- Make sure the student uses the proper form for crossing and uncrossing his or her legs:
  - Jump and cross your legs so that the left foot is on the right side of the midline of your body and the right foot is on the left side of the midline of your body.
  - Jump with legs shoulder width apart, toes pointing forward, knees slightly bent.
  - Cross your legs on first jump, uncross on second jump, cross on third jump, and so on.

Skills Developed

Laterality, motor planning, gross motor coordination

Equipment

- Floor mat
- Wall mat
- Active learning cards (uppercase letters)

Activity

- Floor mat: Jump through the middle row of the mat, landing in each square with your toes alternately pointed inward and outward. While you are stopped, say what is shown on the card for each square.

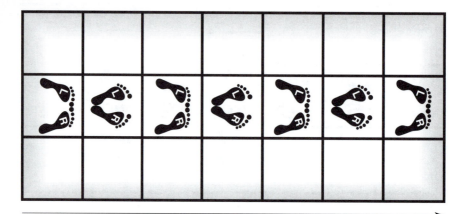

- Wall mat: Starting at the top left, touch the first square with your left hand and at the same time make a fist with your right hand and touch the second square. Cross arms and touch the third square with your right hand (open palm) and the fourth square with your left fist. Repeat on the bottom row going left. Along the way, say what is shown on the card for each square.

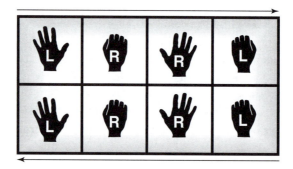

Skill Check

- Encourage the student to speak loudly when saying the uppercase letters.
- Encourage the student to watch his or her foot placement so that both feet end up placed side by side with toes in or out as appropriate.

Skills Developed

Cross-lateral awareness, gross motor coordination

Equipment

Long jump rope

Activity

With the rope on the floor in a straight line, place your left foot on the right side of the rope and your right foot on left side of the rope. Jump, uncrossing your feet in the air, and land with your left foot to the left side of the rope and your right foot to the right side. Say a letter of the alphabet. Jump again, recross your feet in the air, and say the next letter when you land. Continue in this pattern.

Skill Check

Remind the student to slow down and focus on using the correct form for a standing long jump:

- Bend both knees with your arms extended behind your body before takeoff.
- When jumping, thrust your arms forcefully forward and upward (above your head).
- Take off and land with both feet
- Cross your feet on alternating jumps.
- Move your arms downward on landing.

Skills Developed

Laterality, locomotor skills, motor planning

Equipment

- Ladder mat
- Active learning cards (uppercase letters)

Activity

Leap through the mat from rung to rung, switching your lead foot with each leap. Along the way, say what is shown on the card for each square.

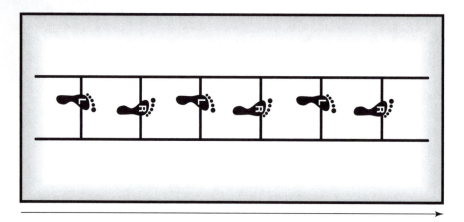

Skill Check

Make sure that the student uses proper form for leaping:

- Move continuously without hesitation before the leap.
- Take off on one foot and land on the other.
- Use a long stride (longer than in running) in which both feet are off the ground during each leap.
- For each leap, reach in front of your body with the arm on the opposite side from your leading (leaping) foot.

Skills Developed

Eye–hand coordination, cross-lateral awareness

Equipment

- Four 30-inch (1-meter) hoops
- Four foam hoop stands

Setup

Place the hoops 2 feet (about half a meter) apart.

Activity

Each time you crawl through a hoop, say the color of the hoop.

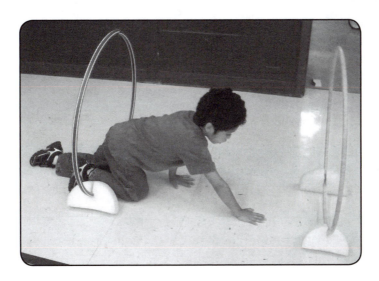

Skill Check

- Encourage the student to be careful not to knock over the hoops.
- Make sure that the student uses proper crawling form:
  - Raise your torso and support your weight on your hands and knees with your stomach off the floor.
  - Move without stopping.
  - Your right hand and left knee (and your left hand and right knee) should move forward simultaneously.
- Encourage student to say the hoop color loudly.

Skills Developed

Laterality, motor planning, gross motor coordination

Equipment

Floor tape

Setup

Use floor tape to make a 6-foot (2-meter) line on the floor.

Activity

Stand with one foot on the line and the other just behind the line. Jump and switch your feet so that you land with the opposite foot on the line. As you jump, say the alphabet, one letter per jump. Try to jump your way through the entire alphabet.

Skill Check

- Make sure that the student switches foot placement by jumping—not merely stepping.
- Remind the student to slow down and focus on using the correct form for a scissor jump:
  - Stand with one foot in front of the other.
  - Jump and switch your feet in the air so that when you land, your other foot is in front.

Skills Developed

Cross-lateral awareness, dynamic balance

Equipment

- Leap, hop, and jump mat
- Floor tape
- Active learning cards (spelling words)

Activity

Start running from a 4-foot (1.2-meter) line 10 feet (3 meters) from the mat and leap across the mat. Leap over the narrow end and work your way to the wide end. Emphasize using good leaping form. On landing, say what is shown on the card for the section of the mat you are leaping over. (This activity is the same as the one for station 8 in weeks 1, 2, 3, and 4 except that it uses different active learning cards.)

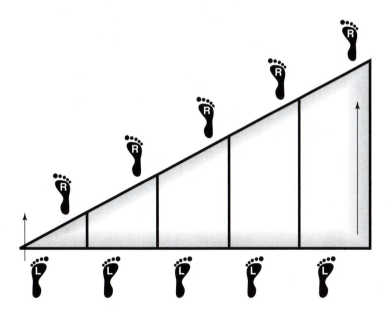

Skill Check

Make sure that the student uses proper form for leaping:

- Move continuously without hesitation before the leap.
- Take off on one foot and land on the other.
- Use a long stride (longer than in running) in which both feet are off the ground during each leap.
- For each leap, reach in front of your body with the arm on the opposite side from your leading (leaping) foot.

Skills Developed

Locomotor skills, motor planning, spatial awareness

Equipment

- Six cones
- Active learning cards (uppercase letters with pictures)

Setup

Place the cones 4 feet (1.2 meter) apart.

Activity

Bear-walk from cone to cone. Along the way, touch each cone and say the letter or picture shown on the card for that cone. (This activity is the same as the one for week 5, station 1.)

Skill Check

- Make sure that the student uses proper form for the bear walk:
  - Bend forward at your waist.
  - Place both hands on the ground.
  - Travel forward slowly.
  - Move the hand and foot on opposite sides of your body at the same time (e.g., left hand, right foot).
- Identify the pictures and have the student identify the sound of the first letter. You may need to help students with this initially, but they will catch on quickly.

Skills Developed

Laterality, locomotor skills, motor planning

Equipment

- Hopscotch mat
- Active learning cards (uppercase letters with pictures)

Activity

Step sideways through the mat, crossing and uncrossing your legs as you move from square to square. At each square, say what is on the card for that square.

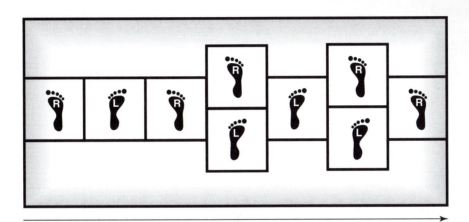

Skill Check

- Make sure that the student crosses or uncrosses his or her legs with each step.
- Make sure the student uses proper form for crossing and uncrossing his or her legs:
  - Step out with the right foot.
  - On the next step, the left foot crosses in back of the right foot.
  - Step out with right foot again and continue by crossing the left foot in back of the right foot and stepping out with the right foot.

Skills Developed

Laterality, motor planning, gross motor coordination

Equipment

- Floor mat
- Wall mat
- Active learning cards (uppercase letters with pictures)

Setup

If you make two sets of the cards, you may use the same card in adjacent squares. If you only have one set of cards, go ahead and put different cards in each square.

Activity

- Floor mat: Do a grapevine step through the middle row of the mat. With each step, say what is shown on the card for that square. To start, stand facing sideways with both feet in the first middle square. Step with your right foot into the second middle square, then step with your left foot into the third square. Next, step again with your right foot, then step again with your left foot. Continue in this way to the end of the mat.

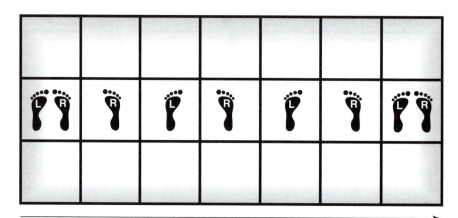

- Wall mat: Start in the upper left corner of the mat. Touch the mat simultaneously with both hands. The left hand touches the mat with the thumb and the right with the index finger. Move to the next two squares switching so that the right hand touches with the thumb and the left with the index finger. Go to the bottom row moving from right to left with the same action. Each time you touch a square, say what is shown on the card for that square.

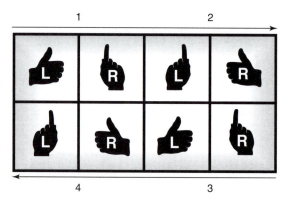

Skill Check

- Encourage the student to speak loudly in saying what is shown on the cards.
- Encourage the student to watch his or her foot placement.

Skills Developed

Laterality, motor planning, gross motor coordination

Equipment

Foo-Foo wands

Activity

Hold a wand in each hand. As you do the activity, use one wand at a time, alternating sides. Use the wand in your right hand to touch parts of your body on the left side. Use the wand in your left hand to touch parts of your body on the right side.

1. Touch the toes of each foot with a wand (first one side, then the other) and say "toes" with each touch.
2. Do the same for your knees and say "knees."
3. Do the same for your shoulders and say "shoulders."
4. Do the same for the sides of your head and say "head."

Skill Check

It may take several days before the student is able to cross the midline of the body effectively, but with practice he or she will get it.

• Concentrate on crossing the vertical midline of the body.
• The right hand only touches body parts on the left side and left hand only touches the right side.

Skills Developed

Gross motor development

Equipment

- Ladder mat
- Active learning cards (uppercase letters with pictures)
- Two cones

Setup

Place the cones 4 feet (1.2 meters) apart and 10 feet (3 meters) from the end of the mat.

Activity

1. Walk through the ladder mat keeping your feet on the rungs. Say what is shown on the active learning cards between the rungs of the ladder mat as you step over them.

2. When you reach the end of the mat, run to the cones. Run between the cones and then return to the beginning of the ladder mat and repeat steps 1 and 2 until it's time to switch stations.

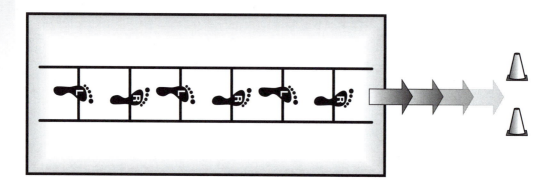

Skill Check

- Make sure that the student uses proper form for walking:
  - Stand tall by keeping your body erect.
  - You should be able to draw a straight line from ear to shoulder.
  - Align your hips, knees, and ankles.
  - Your head should be level and looking forward, and your chin should be parallel to the ground.
  - Your shoulders should be relaxed and your arms bent.
  - Swing your arms in opposition to your foot movement.
  - Walk heel to toe.
- Make sure that the student uses proper form for running:
  - Relax your arms and move them in opposition to your legs with the elbows bent.
  - There is a brief period in which both of your feet are off the ground.
  - Land on your heel or toe (do not run flatfooted).
  - Bend your trailing leg with the heel close to your buttocks.

Skills Developed

Eye–hand coordination, cross-lateral awareness

Equipment

- Stomp board for each student
- One beanbag for each student
- One 13-inch (33-centimeter) paddle for each student

Activity

1. Hold the paddle in your left hand and stomp on the board with your right foot to launch the beanbag into the air. Hit the beanbag with the paddle.

2. Retrieve your beanbag and repeat the activity but this time stomp with your left foot and hold the paddle with your right hand. Hit the beanbag with the paddle. Repeat steps 1 and 2 until you have done each side 5 times.

(This activity is the same as the one for week 4, station 6, except that this time the student does not say letters.)

Skill Check

- Make sure that the student uses proper form for cross-lateral stomping:
  - Face the board with your feet slightly apart and adjacent to each other.
  - Step quickly on the stomp board with minimum force (not too hard).
  - If stomping with your right foot, use the paddle with your left hand; if stomping with your left foot, use the paddle with your right hand.
- Caution the student to neither run and stomp nor jump and stomp because the board may slide causing the student to slip and fall. Also the movement is more controlled when the stomp is not accompanied with a run or jump.

Skills Developed

Spatial awareness, gross motor coordination

Equipment

- Scooter board
- Two cones
- Two cone covers
- Active learning cards (uppercase letters with pictures)

Setup

Position two cones with active learning cards 10 feet (3 meters) apart.

Activity

Lie on your tummy on the scooter board and move yourself around the cones in an oval pattern. In moving yourself, alternate using a foot and hand on opposite sides of your body—first your right hand and left foot, then your left hand and right foot. Each time you pass a cone, say the letter shown on the card for that cone.

Skill Check

- Stress scooter board safety (e.g., never stand on the board, keep hands on the side, keep hair and clothing away from the wheels).
- Watch for cross-laterality, making sure the student uses his or her left hand and right foot or right hand and left foot to propel the scooter.
- Make sure the student speaks aloud what is shown on the cards.

Skills Developed

Cross-lateral awareness, dynamic balance

Equipment

- Leap, hop, and jump mat
- Floor tape
- Active learning cards (spelling words)

Activity

Start from a line 10 feet (3 meters) from the mat and leap across the mat. Start at the narrow end and work your way to the wide end. Emphasize using good leaping form. On landing, say what is shown on the card for the section of the mat you are leaping over. (This activity is the same as the one for station 8 in weeks 1, 2, 3, 4, and 5 except that it uses different active learning cards.)

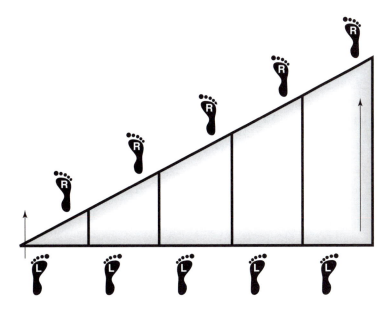

Skill Check

Make sure that the student uses proper form for leaping:

- Move continuously without hesitation before the leap.
- Take off on one foot and land on the other.
- Use a long stride (longer than in running) in which both feet are off the ground during each leap.
- For each leap, reach in front of your body with the arm on the opposite side from your leading (leaping) foot.

Skills Developed

Locomotor skills, motor planning, spatial awareness

Equipment

- Six cones
- Active learning cards (uppercase letters with pictures)

Setup

Place the cones 4 feet (1.2 meters) apart in a straight line.

Activity

Walk from cone to cone. Along the way, touch each cone and say the letter or picture shown on the card for that cone.

Skill Check

- Make sure that the student uses proper form for walking:
    - Stand tall by keeping your body erect.
    - You should be able to draw a straight line from ear to shoulder.
    - Align your hips, knees, and ankles.
    - Your head should be level and looking forward, and your chin should be parallel to the ground.
    - Your shoulders should be relaxed and your arms bent.
    - Swing your arms in opposition to your foot movement.
    - Walk heel to toe.
- Identify the pictures and have the student identify the sound of the first letter. You may need to help students with this initially, but they will catch on quickly.

Skills Developed

Laterality, locomotor skills, motor planning

Equipment

- Hopscotch mat
- Active learning cards (lowercase letters and spelling words)

Activity

Leap from square to square through the hopscotch mat. When you arrive at side-by-side squares, cross your feet as you leap. As you go through the mat, say what is shown on the card for each square you pass.

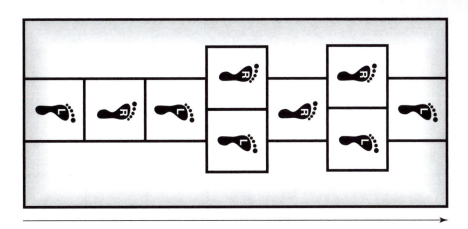

Skill Check

- Make sure that the student uses proper form for leaping:
  - Move continuously without hesitation before the leap.
  - Take off on one foot and land on the other.
  - Use a long stride (longer than in running) in which both feet are off the ground during each leap.
  - For each leap, reach in front of your body with the arm on the opposite side from your leading (leaping) foot.
- Make sure that the student places his or her feet as shown in the diagram in order to cross feet in the side-by-side squares.

Skills Developed

Laterality, motor planning, gross motor coordination

Equipment

- Floor mat
- Wall mat
- One beanbag for each student
- Active learning cards (lowercase letters with spelling words)

Activity

- Floor mat: Toss a beanbag into a square (your choice), then leap to the square behind it and say what is shown on the card in the square the beanbag is on. Continue tossing the beanbag and leaping to it until you get to the end of the mat. If your toss lands outside the mat, retrieve the beanbag and try again.

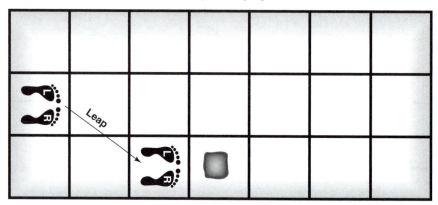

- Wall mat: For this activity, use the four center squares of the wall mat. Lift one knee and use your opposite hand to touch the square opposite your hand. For example, lift your left knee and use your right hand to touch the upper left square of the center four squares. Then switch: Lift your right knee and use your left hand to touch 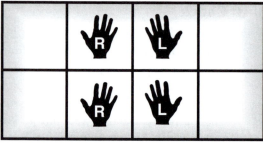 upper right square of the center four. Each time you touch a square, say what is shown on the card for that square.

Lift opposite knee when touching mat

Skill Check

- Encourage the student to speak loudly in saying what is shown in each card.
- Make sure that the student uses proper form for leaping:
  - Move continuously without hesitation before the leap.
  - Take off on one foot and land on the other.
  - Use a long stride in which both feet are off the ground during each leap.
  - For each leap, reach in front of your body with the arm on the opposite side from your leading (leaping) foot.
- Make sure that the student uses proper form for the underhand toss:
  - Face the target. Step with the foot on the opposite side from your throwing hand. Bring your arm back, then swing it forward and release the ball.

Skills Developed

Dynamic balance, cross-laterality, motor planning, coordination

Equipment

- Bucket stilts
- Four cones
- Active learning cards (lowercase letters and spelling words)

Setup

Place the cones in a row, 2 feet (about half a meter) apart.

Activity

1. Walk through the cones with a bucket stilt on your left foot while holding the stilt rope with your right hand. For each cone, say the lowercase letter shown on the card.

2. Repeat with the bucket stilt on your right foot while holding the stilt rope with your left hand.

Skill Check

Make sure that the student holds the rope with the hand on the opposite side from the foot walking on the stilt. The student may need practice in order to get the cross-lateral idea.

Skills Developed

Gross motor development

Equipment

- Ladder mat
- Active learning cards (lowercase letters and spelling words)

Activity

Crawl through the ladder mat to the end. As you pass each square, say what is shown on the card for that square.

Skill Check

Make sure that the student uses proper crawling form:

- Raise your torso and support your weight on your hands and knees with your stomach off the floor.
- Move without stopping.
- Your right hand and left knee (and your left hand and right knee) should move forward simultaneously.

Skills Developed

Spatial awareness, gross motor coordination

Equipment

- Scooter board
- 15-foot (4.5-meter) jump rope
- Volleyball standard or other apparatus

Setup

Attach the rope to the base of the volleyball standard or similar apparatus and lay it (fully extended) on the floor. Position the scooter at the free end of the rope.

Activity

Lie on your tummy on the scooter board. Alternate using your right hand and your left hand to pull yourself along the rope. As you move along, recite the alphabet.

Skill Check

- Stress scooter board safety (e.g., never stand on the board, keep hands on the side, keep hair and clothing away from the wheels).
- Watch for cross-laterality, making sure the student alternates his or her hands.
- Encourage the student to say the alphabet loudly.

Skills Developed

Eye–hand coordination, cross-lateral awareness

Equipment

One juggling scarf for each student

Activity

Toss the scarf up with your right hand and catch it with your left hand. Then toss it with your left hand and catch it with your right hand. Count each catch aloud.

Skill Check

- Make sure that the student uses one hand to toss and the other to catch.
- Make sure that the student uses proper form for the lion's claw catch:
  - Prepare by extending your hand in front of your body with your elbow bent and your palm facing outward.
  - Reach for the object by moving your hand downward with the palm facing down.
  - Catch the object with your hand only—not against your leg or thigh.
  - While catching, keep your eyes on the object.
- Emphasize safety: The scarf is very slippery when it is on the floor. Instruct the student to keep the scarf off of the floor.

Skills Developed

Cross-lateral awareness, dynamic balance

Equipment

- Ten poly spots
- Active learning cards (spelling words)

Setup

Place the poly spots on the floor as shown in the diagram. They should be in two rows and 6 inches (15 centimeters) from each other. Attach active learning cards to each poly spot with a piece of Velcro.

Activity

1. Walk forward on your toes from one poly spot to another, putting the right foot on the spot on the right side and the left foot on the spot on the left side. At each poly spot, say the word shown on the card. Continue until you reach the end of the sequence. Repeat the activity but this time walk backward on your toes.

2. Walk forward on your heels from one poly spot to another, putting the right foot on the spot on the right and the left foot on the spot on the left. At each poly spot, say the word shown on the card. Continue until you reach the end of the sequence.

Skill Check

- Stress foot placement and form.
- Make sure that the student uses proper form for walking:
  - Stand tall by keeping your body erect.
  - You should be able to draw a straight line from ear to shoulder.
  - Align your hips, knees, and ankles.
  - Your head should be level and looking forward, and your chin should be parallel to the ground.
  - Your shoulders should be relaxed and your arms bent.
  - Swing your arms in opposition to your foot movement.
  - Walk heel to toe.
- Make sure that the student does not kick the poly spots out of position by stressing walking and placing foot on the middle of the spot.

Skills Developed

Locomotor skills, motor planning, spatial awareness

Equipment

- Six cones
- Active learning cards (uppercase letters with pictures)

Setup

Place the cones 4 feet (1.2 meter) apart.

Activity

Bear-walk from cone to cone. Along the way, touch each cone and say the letter or picture shown on the card for that cone. (This activity is the same as the one for station 1 in weeks 5 and 6.)

Skill Check

- Make sure that the student uses proper form for the bear walk:
  - Bend forward at your waist.
  - Place both hands on the ground.
  - Travel forward slowly.
  - Move the hand and foot on opposite sides of your body at the same time (e.g., left hand, right foot).
- Identify the pictures and have the student identify the sound of the first letter. You may need to help students with this initially, but they will catch on quickly.

Skills Developed

Laterality, locomotor skills, motor planning

Equipment

- Hopscotch mat
- Active learning cards (uppercase letters and spelling words)

Activity

Walk beside the mat and bounce the ball twice in each square, skipping the farther square when you get to the two pairs. In bouncing the ball, alternate using your left hand and your right hand in every other square. For each square, say what is shown on the card.

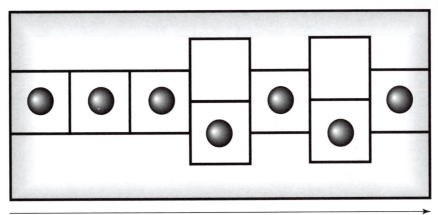

Bounce the ball twice in each square

Skill Check

- Make sure that the student walks beside the mat.
- Make sure that the student uses proper form for walking:
  - Stand tall by keeping your body erect.
  - You should be able to draw a straight line from ear to shoulder.
  - Align your hips, knees, and ankles.
  - Your head should be level and looking forward, and your chin should be parallel to the ground.
  - Your shoulders should be relaxed and your arms bent.
  - Swing your arms in opposition to your foot movement.
  - Walk heel to toe.
- Make sure that the student alternates hands in bouncing the ball.
- Make sure that the student uses proper form for dribbling:
  - Keep your eyes up.
  - Use your finger pads—not your fingertips.
  - For good control, dribble at your side and at waist level or lower.
  - Dribble the ball in your "foot pocket" created by dropping your right foot behind your left foot (or vice versa if using left hand).

Skills Developed

Laterality, motor planning, gross motor coordination

Equipment

- Floor mat
- Wall mat
- One beanbag for each student
- Active learning cards (uppercase letters and spelling words)

Activity

- Floor mat: Toss a beanbag onto a square of your choice and move to the square behind it in a hopscotch pattern (e.g., hop, jump, hop, jump). As you move through the squares, say what is shown on each card you pass.

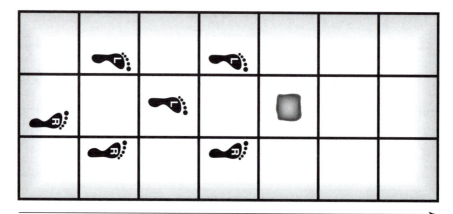

- Wall mat: Begin at the top left side of the wall mat, touching the first two squares. Move to the next two squares to the right, crossing hands while crossing feet at the same time. Uncross hands and feet and place hands in the two squares on the bottom right of the mat. Then cross hands and feet again and touch the bottom right squares of the wall mat. Each time you touch the mat, say what is shown on the cards.

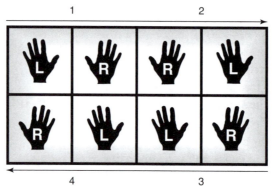

When hands are crossed, feet should be crossed

Skill Check

- Encourage the student to speak loudly in saying the letters in the squares.
- Encourage the student to watch his or her foot placement, making sure his or her feet are crossed and uncrossed appropriately.

Skills Developed

Cross-pattern awareness, gross motor coordination

Equipment

- White and black foam bricks (4 of each)
- Floor tape

Setup

Use floor tape to make a 10-foot (3-meter) line on the floor. Arrange two rows of bricks 1 foot (30 centimeters) away from the line (one on either side of the tape line)—the right one containing white bricks and the left one containing black bricks. In each row, the bricks should be 2 feet (about half a meter) apart. Stagger the spacing of the two rows as shown in the illustration. Mark each brick's position with a small piece of tape to provide a guide for resetting the bricks after they are kicked over.

Activity

Walk forward on the line, knocking down black bricks on the left side with your right foot and knocking down white bricks on the right side with your left foot. Return to your starting point by walking back along the line. As you go, set up the bricks on each side of the line with the hand on the opposite side of your body.

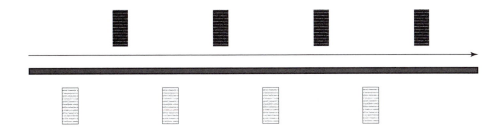

Skill Check

Make sure that the student kicks with the foot on the opposite side from the bricks and moves the foot across the midline of his or her body.

Skills Developed

Gross motor development

Equipment

- Ladder mat
- Active learning cards (uppercase letters and spelling words)

Activity

Crawl backward through the ladder mat to the end. As you pass each square, say what is shown on the card for that square.

Skill Check

- Make sure that the student uses proper crawling form:
  - Raise your torso and support your weight on your hands and knees with your stomach off the floor.
  - Move without stopping.
  - Your right hand and left knee (and your left hand and right knee) should move forward simultaneously.
- Encourage the student to say aloud what is shown on each card.

Skills Developed

Eye–hand coordination, cross-lateral awareness

Equipment

- One 8.5-inch (22-centimeter) playground ball for each student
- Four cones
- Active learning cards (uppercase letters and spelling words)

Setup

Place the cones in a row about 1 foot (30 centimeters) from the wall with 4 feet (1.2 meters) between each cone.

Activity

1. From a line 10 feet (3 meters) away from the row of cones, read what is shown on the cards. Then roll the ball between the cones, stepping with the foot on the opposite side from the rolling hand.

2. Read what is shown on the cards and then roll the ball and try to hit the cone, stepping with your right foot and rolling with your left hand or stepping with your left foot and rolling with your right hand. If you knock over your cone, reset it as you retrieve your ball. Repeat steps 1 and 2 as long as the station music is on.

Skill Check

Make sure that the student uses proper form for rolling:

- Face your target.
- Step with your opposite foot toward the target (e.g., if rolling with your right hand, step with your left foot, or vice versa).
- Use a pendulum motion with your arm to roll the ball (as in bowling).
- Bend your knees to lower your body and release the ball close to the ground.
- Follow through with your rolling hand toward the sky or ceiling.

CROSS-LATERAL ACTIVITIES

Skills Developed

Spatial awareness, gross motor coordination

Equipment

6-foot (2-meter) tumbling mat

Activity

Crawl to the end of the mat, then crab-walk back as fast as possible. Recite the alphabet throughout the activity.

Skill Check

- Make sure that the student uses proper crawling form:
  - Raise your torso and support your weight on your hands and knees with your stomach off the floor.
  - Move without stopping.
  - Your right hand and left knee (and your left hand and right knee) should move forward simultaneously.
- Make sure that the student uses proper form for the crab walk:
  - With your back toward the floor, support yourself on your hands and feet.
  - Your arms should be bent and your buttocks off the floor.
  - Move your feet in opposition to your arms (e.g., move left foot with right arm).
  - Move continually and smoothly.

Skills Developed

Cross-lateral awareness, locomotor skills

Equipment

- Leap, hop, and jump mat
- Floor tape
- Active learning cards (spelling words)

Activity

Start running at a 6-foot (2-meter) line 10 feet (3 meters) from the mat and leap across the mat. Start at the narrow end and work your way to the wide end. Emphasize using good leaping form. On landing, say what is shown on the card for the section of the mat you are leaping over. (This activity is the same as the one for station 8 in weeks 1, 2, 3, 4, 5, and 6 except that it uses different active learning cards.)

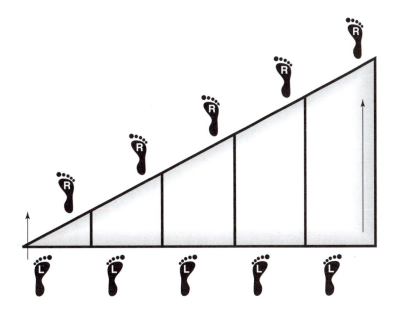

Skill Check

Make sure that the student uses proper form for leaping:

- Move continuously without hesitation before the leap.
- Take off on one foot and land on the other.
- Use a long stride (longer than in running) in which both feet are off the ground during each leap.
- For each leap, reach in front of your body with the arm on the opposite side from your leading (leaping) foot.

5

COMBINATION ACTIVITIES

These combined stations provide a culmination for the motor laboratory. The activities included here review all three lateralities: bilaterality, unilaterality, and cross-laterality.

Skills Developed

Laterality, locomotor skills, motor planning

Equipment

- Jump box (12 inches [30 centimeters] high)
- One foam hurdle (made by balancing a pool noodle on two cones for support)
- Three hoops (two for the floor, one with a stand)

Setup

Place the hurdle 12 inches (30 centimeters) in front of the jump box. Place the first hoop 12 inches (30 centimeters) in front of the hurdle and the second hoop 12 inches (30 centimeters) from the first hoop. Set up the third hoop in the stand and place it 2 feet (0.6 meters) in front of the second hoop.

Activity

1. Step onto the box.
2. Jump from the box over the hurdle and into hoop 1.
3. Jump from hoop 1 to hoop 2.
4. Step through the last hoop.

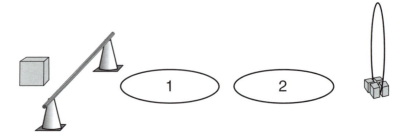

Skill Check

- Make sure that only one child is on the course at a time.
- Be sure students prepare to jump with movement that includes bending both of their knees and extending their arms behind the body.

Skills Developed

Locomotor skills, motor planning, eye–hand coordination

Equipment

- Mini trampoline (37 inches [about a meter])
- Scooter board
- 6-foot (2-meter) jump rope
- Hoop
- 8.5-inch (22-centimeter) playground ball

Setup

Place the scooter board 4 feet (1.2 meters) in front of the mini trampoline. Place the jump rope 5 feet (1.5 meters) in front of the scooter board and the hoop and ball 4 feet (1.2 meters) in front of the jump rope.

Activity

1. Jump on the mini trampoline 5 times.
2. Lie facing forward on your tummy on the scooter board and use both arms together to propel yourself forward to the rope.
3. Jump over the rope from front to back and then back to front five times.
4. Walk to the hoop and bounce the ball in the hoop five times with both hands together.

Skill Check

- Emphasize safety.
  - Stress scooter board safety (e.g., never stand on the board, keep hands on the side, keep hair and clothing away from the wheels).
  - Remind the student to watch where he or she is going and to avoid stepping on the rope.
  - Remind students to stop jumping on the trampoline and then step off to go to the next piece of equipment; they should not jump off the trampoline.
- Remind the student to slow down and focus on using the correct form for a standing long jump:
  - Bend both knees with your arms extended behind your body before takeoff.
  - When jumping, thrust your arms forcefully forward and upward (above your head).
  - Take off and land with both feet.
  - Move your arms downward on landing.
- Students should use both hands to push the ball to the ground.

Skills Developed

Cross-lateral awareness, dynamic balance, eye–hand coordination

Equipment

- Ladder mat
- Three hoops
- Stomp board
- One beanbag

Setup

Place the hoops in a row 4 feet (1.2 meters) away from the ladder mat with 1 foot (30 centimeters) in between each one. The stompboard should be placed 4 feet (1.2 meters) away from the last hoop.

Activity

1. Walk on the rungs of the ladder.
2. Leap into and then out of each hoop.
3. Stomp on the board with your right foot to launch the beanbag, then catch it with your left hand.
4. Stomp on the board with your left foot to launch the beanbag, then catch it with your right hand.

Skill Check

- Stress safety.
  - Caution the student to neither run and stomp nor jump and stomp because the board may slide, causing the student to slip and fall. Also the movement is more controlled when the stomp is not accompanied with a run or jump.
  - Remind students not to hurry through the course.
- Make sure that the student uses proper form for leaping:
  - Move continuously without hesitation before the leap.
  - Take off on one foot and land on the other.
  - Use a long stride (longer than in running) in which both feet are off the ground during each leap.
  - For each leap, reach in front of your body with the arm on the opposite side from your leading (leaping) foot.

Skills Developed

Cross-lateral awareness, dynamic balance, eye–hand coordination

Equipment

- Scooter board
- 10-foot (3-meter) tunnel
- Three cones
- Two noodles or long jump ropes 14 feet (about 4 meters) in length

Activity

1. Lie on your tummy on the scooter board. Use alternating hands to propel yourself forward through the tunnel.
2. Kneel on the scooter board and use alternate hands to weave through the cones.
3. Sit on the scooter board and use alternating feet to propel yourself backward through the space between the noodles or ropes.

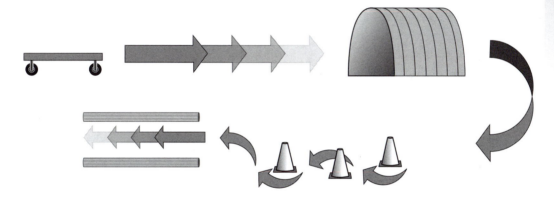

Skill Check

- Stress scooter board safety (e.g., never stand on the board, keep hands on the side, keep hair and clothing away from the wheels).
- Make sure that the student uses only one hand at a time in propelling the scooter board.

Skills Developed

Eye–hand coordination, unilateral awareness

Equipment

- Foam geometric shapes or active learning cards (shapes)
- 8.5-inch (22-centimeter) playground ball

Setup

Place the shapes or cards 4 feet (1.2 meters) apart to allow space for students to hop to the next shape or card.

Activity

Hop from shape to shape or from card to card. At each shape or card, bounce the ball in the shape five times with your right hand and five times with your left hand. While bouncing the ball, say the shape and color.

Skill Check

- The student may try to bounce the ball with two hands; if so, encourage him or her to use the indicated hand.
- Make sure that the student uses proper form for dribbling:
  - Keep your eyes up.
  - Use your finger pads—not your fingertips.
  - For good control, dribble at your side and at waist level or lower.
  - Dribble the ball in your "foot pocket" created by dropping your right foot behind your left foot (or vice versa if using left hand).
- Make sure that the student uses proper hopping form:
  - Swing your non-weight-bearing leg like a pendulum to produce power.
  - On landing, keep the foot of your non-weight-bearing leg behind your body.
  - Bend your arms and swing them forward to produce power.

Skills Developed

Eye–hand coordination, motor planning, dynamic balance

Equipment

- Eight hoops
- Floor beam
- 8.5-inch (22-centimeter) playground ball

Setup

Set each hoop close enough to the floor beam so the students can bounce the ball in the hoop as they slide down the beam.

Activity

1. Hop five times in each hoop.
2. Get on the beam and slide sideways to the right to the end of the beam. As you go, bounce the ball once in each hoop with your right hand.
3. Return to the starting end of the beam by sliding sideways to the left. As you go, bounce the ball once in each hoop with your left hand.

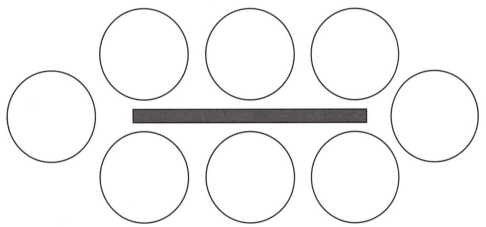

Skill Check

- Emphasize safety—make sure that only one child is on the beam at a time.
- If the student has trouble with walking on the beam, he or she may walk on a tape line on the floor.
- Make sure that the student uses proper hopping form:
  - Swing your non-weight-bearing leg like a pendulum to produce power.
  - On landing, keep the foot of your non-weight-bearing leg behind your body.
  - Bend your arms and swing them forward to produce power.
- Make sure that the student uses proper sliding form:
  - Turn your body sideways.
  - Step sideways with your leading foot, then slide your trailing foot to meet it.
  - Move with a rhythmic continual motion.
- Make sure that the student uses proper form for dribbling:
  - Keep your eyes up.
  - Use your finger pads—not your fingertips.
  - For good control, dribble at your side, at waist level or lower, and in your "foot pocket" created by dropping your right foot behind your left foot (or vice versa if using left hand).

Skills Developed

Bilateral awareness, eye–hand coordination, motor planning

Equipment

- Three hoops
- Scooter board
- Beanbag
- Floor tape

Setup

Place the hoops in a line so that they are touching each other. Use the floor tape to mark an X 2 feet (about half a meter) away from the hoops and place the scooter there. Place the beanbag 6 feet (2 meters) away from the scooter board.

Activity

1. Jump from hoop to hoop by taking off and landing with both feet simultaneously.
2. Lie on your tummy on the scooter board and use both hands at the same time to propel yourself forward to the beanbag.
3. Get off the scooter board.
4. Toss and catch the beanbag five times with both hands at the same time.
5. Place the scooter back on the piece of tape for the next person to use.

Beanbag

Skill Check

- Stress scooter board safety (e.g., never stand on the board, keep hands on the side, keep hair and clothing away from the wheels).
- Remind the student to focus on using the correct form for a standing long jump:
  - Bend both knees with your arms extended behind your body before takeoff.
  - When jumping, thrust your arms forcefully forward and upward.
  - Take off and land with both feet.
  - Move your arms downward on landing.
- Make sure that the student uses proper form for tossing:
  - Use both hands together to make the toss.
  - Make your tosses equally high.
  - Keep your eyes focused at the peak of the toss.
  - Keep your elbows close to your body.
  - Stand straight without leaning.
- Make sure that the student uses proper form for catching:
  - Reach for the object as it approaches you.
  - Catch the object with your hands only—not against your chest.
  - Keep your eyes on the object.
  - If the object is below your waist, keep your pinkies together.
  - If the object is above your waist, keep your thumbs together.

Skills Developed

Cross-lateral awareness, motor planning

Equipment

- Incline mat
- Step box (12 inches [30 centimeters] high)
- Hoop on floor
- Hoop on stand
- Hurdle on two cones

Setup

Place one hoop on the floor 1 foot (30 centimeters) in front of the incline mat. The vertical hoop should be set up 4 feet (1.2 meters) away from the hoop on the floor. Place the hurdle 4 feet (1.2 meters) away from the vertical hoop.

Activity

1. Crawl up the incline mat onto the step box.
2. Jump off of the box into the hoop on the floor.
3. Step through the vertical hoop and say "through."
4. Crawl under the hurdle and say "under."

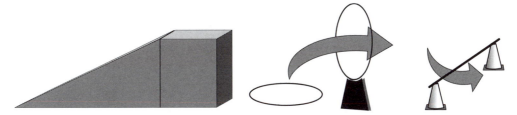

Skill Check

- Stress safety—only one child may be on the incline mat and step box at a time.
- Make sure that the student uses proper crawling form:
  - Raise your torso and support your weight on your hands and knees with your stomach off the floor.
  - Move without stopping.
  - Your right hand and left knee (and your left hand and right knee) should move forward simultaneously.
- Remind the student to slow down and focus on using the correct form for a standing long jump:
  - Bend both knees with your arms extended behind your body before takeoff.
  - When jumping, thrust your arms forcefully forward and upward (above your head).
  - Take off and land with both feet.
  - Move your arms downward on landing.

GLOSSARY

agility—ability to start, stop, and change direction without losing one's balance

balance—ability to make continuous and accurate adjustments of the body (when moving—dynamic balance; when stationary—static balance)

bilateral movement—activity in which one does the same thing at the same time with both sides of the body

body awareness—knowledge of one's body parts, what one's body looks like, and one's capabilities and limitations

cross-lateral movement—activity in which one moves opposite sides of the body at the same time (e.g., using right arm and left leg to crawl)

directionality—ability to move in a variety of directions (e.g., up, down, through, around) as instructed

kinesthetic awareness—awareness of one's body in space while moving or stationary

laterality—control of some physical or mental function by one side of the body or either hemisphere of the brain

motor planning—the ability to think through and physically carry out a task

perceptual-motor skill—skill that involves receiving information through sensory input systems (reflexive, visual, tactile, vestibular, kinesthetic)

spatial relation ability—ability to perceive the position of objects in space as they relate to the position of one's body

tactile awareness—receipt of information by directly touching and feeling an object

temporal awareness—awareness of the passage of time, which is essential for a sense of rhythm

unilateral movement—movement using one side of the body

BIBLIOGRAPHY

Belknap, Martha. *Mind and Body Magic.* Duluth, MN: Whole Person Associates, 1997.

Brehm, Madeline, and Nancy Tindell. *Movement With a Purpose.* West Nyack, CA: Parker, 1983.

Caine, Geoffrey. *Making Connections—Teaching the Human Brain.* Alexandria, VA: Association for Supervision and Curriculum Development, 1991.

Capon, Jack. *Perceptual-Motor Lesson Plans Level 1.* Alameda, CA: Front Row Experience, 1998.

Dennison, Paul. *Brain Gym.* Ventura, CA: Edu-Kinesthetics, 1988.

Hannaford, Carla. *Smart Moves.* Atlanta, GA: Great Oceans Publishers, 1995.

———. *The Dominance Factor.* Arlington, VA: Great Oceans Publishers, 1997.

Jensen, Eric. *The Learning Brain.* San Diego, CA: The Brain Store, 1995.

———. *Amazing Brain Facts.* San Diego, CA: The Brain Store, 1997.

———. *Learning With the Body in Mind.* San Diego, CA: The Brain Store, 2000.

Strauss, Robert. *The Teaching of Developmental Movement Skills.* San Antonio, TX: Trinity University, n.d.

ABOUT THE AUTHORS

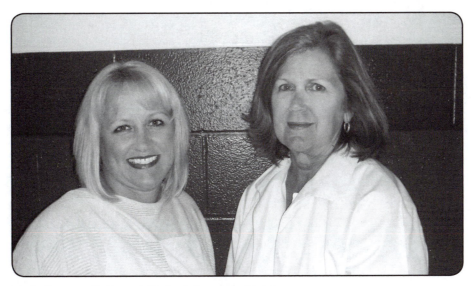

Molly Ramon (left) and Jill A. Johnstone (right).

Jill A. Johnstone and **Molly Ramon** are elementary physical education teachers in San Antonio, Texas. Between the two of them, they have nearly 50 years of experience teaching physical education as well as 7 years of research, development, and implementation of perceptual-motor learning laboratories in public school settings. They have made presentations and taught workshops on the perceptual-motor activities program at the district, state, and national levels.

Their program has been tested in public schools and reviewed by professors at the University of Texas at San Antonio. Jill and Molly have trained teachers and monitored labs at more than 45 schools, assisting with the implementation of the program. They are members of the Texas Association for Health, Physical Education, Recreation and Dance and the American Alliance for Health, Physical Education, Recreation and Dance. Jill enjoys reading, hiking, and kayaking; Molly enjoys coaching, reading, and spending time with her family.

You'll find other outstanding
physical education resources at
www.HumanKinetics.com

In the U.S. call 1.800.747.4457
Australia 08 8372 0999
Canada. 1.800.465.7301
Europe . . . . . +44 (0) 113 255 5665
New Zealand . . . 0064 9 448 1207

HUMAN KINETICS
The Information Leader in Physical Activity
P.O. Box 5076 • Champaign, IL 61825-5076